The
COPYRIGHT HANDBOOK

The
COPYRIGHT
HANDBOOK
for Fine and Applied Arts

BY HOWARD WALLS

WATSON-GUPTILL PUBLICATIONS

NEW YORK

THE PURPOSE OF THIS BOOK

Most persons do not understand legalistics, or do not want to, and there is no reason to believe that artists and composers are exceptions to this common truth.

This book is planned to give you a broad, not bored, perspective of copyright. It deals succinctly with copyright as it is today—stripped of its legal jargon but not its meaning. An ordinary reading of these contents will provide you with a comprehensive, satisfying, and enviable knowledge of copyright—free of confused and unintelligible talk—and will put you in a commanding position at all times in the marketing of your work.

HOWARD WALLS

Washington, D. C.
December 22, 1962

THANK YOU

MR. WILLIAM SIEGFRIED
Assistant Register of Copyrights
  For your official and personal courtesies.

MR. BENJAMIN RUDD
Copyright Office Attorney-Adviser-Librarian
  For your help in preparing the bibliography.

MR. LOUIS SMITH
Copyright Office Counsel
  For supplying me with much of the bibliographical material.

MR. ALAN LATMAN
Executive Secretary and Counsel
National Committee for Effective Design Legislation
  For your help with the protection problems in the
  field of applied art.

MR. HERMAN FINKELSTEIN
General Counsel
American Society of Composers, Authors, and Publishers (ASCAP)
  For your help with the protection problems in the field of music.

MR. COURTNEY PACE
Administrative Assistant
U. S. Senator James O. Eastland
Chairman, Senate Committee on the Judiciary
  For your help with the Committee studies on copyright.

MR. OSCAR E. MOLLARI
A friend who never fails
  For the many ways you helped in the preparation of this book.

CONTENTS

PART ONE: THE ABC OF COPYRIGHT

PART TWO: ART COPYRIGHT

PART THREE: MUSIC COPYRIGHT

SOURCES OF INFORMATION

This book is a nontechnical digest embracing subject matter selected and edited from United States statutes and treaties, congressional reports, presidential proclamations, federal regulations and rules of practice, federal court decisions, articles of international conventions, copyright studies of the U. S. Senate Committee on the Judiciary, reports of the Register of Copyrights, and various official government publications and bulletins relating to copyright.

Part One

THE ABC OF COPYRIGHT

ON COPYRIGHT IN GENERAL
A Very Important Note

As a creator of fine or applied art, you are probably interested in only the specifics of art or music copyright which are presented in Parts II and III of this book. There are, however, many rules of copyright which apply equally to works of literature, science and art, and a knowledge of these is essential to your legal protection. These rules are presented here, in Part I, to enhance your copyright knowledge in your special field.

EXPLANATION OF THE WORD "AUTHOR"

The word "author," as used throughout this presentation of general copyright rules, is not limited simply to one who writes a book. It is used, necessarily, in its broadest sense—meaning the beginner or prime mover of anything, an originator, a creator. Hence *the word includes artist and composer.*

An author may be an individual, a firm or partnership, a corporation, or an association or other collective group legally capable of holding and defending property.

The word "author" includes not only authors of original works but also translators, editors, compilers, illustrators, adapters, arrangers, and the like.

THE COPYRIGHT OFFICE

Before we explore the meaning and importance of "copyright," let us take a quick look at the Copyright Office and the many ways in which it is organized to serve you effectively in the protection of your intellectual property.

First off, there is a general public misconception that the Copyright Office *issues* copyrights.

3

Copyright is a ready-made grant by the United States Government, which may be *claimed* by an author who, in effect, secures his own copyright by complying with certain simple formalities.

Consequently, *the Copyright Office is primarily an office of record which records claims to copyright.*

Registration Services

Registering a claim to copyright is a simple matter which may be done by the claimant himself, without legal aid or expense.

In the process of securing your own copyright, you will be corresponding or dealing directly with the Copyright Office.

The Copyright Office is a department of The Library of Congress. The administrative head of the department is called the Register of Copyrights.

All transactions with the Copyright Office may be addressed:

> **The Register of Copyrights**
> **Copyright Office**
> **The Library of Congress**
> **Washington 25, D. C.**

The Copyright Office offers you a public service:

It will send to you on request, without cost, the proper form on which your application for copyright will be made.

It is ready to aid you as a copyright applicant orally, or by correspondence, in the formal presentation of your application.

It will determine whether your application and the materials deposited by you for copyright meet the requirements of the law, and will advise you of any further steps you might need to take to protect your claim in a particular case.

4

Custodial Services

The custodial services of the Office include the orderly maintenance of records, correspondence, index files, and such copies of copyright deposits as are preserved in the Office.

The ultimate purpose aimed at, of course, is the preservation of evidence to support claims of copyright. Records of the distant past, beyond the span of copyright, naturally tend to lose their strictly legal importance and become merged in the mass of material of general cultural significance preserved by The Library of Congress; but during the life of copyright, the maintenance of the record is of great legal importance.

Informative Services

The Copyright Office is the chief source of information regarding all recorded claims to copyright from 1790 to date. This information is furnished in search reports, in the published cumulative *Catalog of Copyright Entries,* and in various informational bulletins and circulars.

The Office provides a copyright reference service for members of Congress, attorneys, authors, publishers, corporations, government agencies, and the general public in all copyright subjects involving several million registered claims.

It assists and advises attorneys and government and private investigators in the use of Copyright Office facilities, and suggests sources helpful in research.

The searches made by the Office range from simple inquiries as to the date of copyright of a single item, through long and complicated searches, some of which involve hundreds of registrations and assignments of copyright.

Assignments, which may be recorded in the Office, make up the complete record of an author's property. Such records are used

5

by attorneys, authors, publishers, and others, in this country and abroad, in the settlement of estates and in cases of copyright litigation.

Searches of the records, indexes, and deposits are made on request. There is a fee of three dollars per hour for such information.

The Copyright Office is prevented by law from furnishing applicants with legal advice concerning their problems. This is particularly true of questions involving possible infringement, which would ordinarily have to be decided by a court.

Nor is it possible for the Office to furnish opinions on the merits of any particular work, to recommend publishers, lawyers, music writers or agents, or to advise applicants as to their contractual arrangements.

WHAT IS COPYRIGHT?

Copyright, as the inverse of the word implies, literally means the *right to copy.* It is the right of an author to control the reproduction of his intellectual creation.

As long as an author keeps his work in his sole possession, his absolute control of it is a physical fact and his rights are protected by the common law. When he discloses the work to others, however, he makes it possible for them to reproduce it. Copyright is a legal device to give him the right to control its reproduction after it has been disclosed.

Copyright does not preclude others from using the ideas or subject matter revealed by the author's work. It pertains to the literary, musical, graphic, or artistic form in which the author expresses intellectual concepts. It enables him to prevent others from reproducing his original and individual expression.

Thus an artist may paint his conception of the sinking of the *Titanic,* but this will not preclude another artist from painting his own version of the same event; a composer may write a musical

6

interpretation of the annual fair at Nizhnii Novgorod, but this will not preclude another composer from writing one just as noisy.

Anyone is free to create his own expression of another's concepts or to make practical use of them, if he does not copy the *form of expression.*

Copyright as Property

Copyright is generally regarded as a form of property, but it is property of a unique kind. While it is intangible and incorporeal, the thing to which the property attaches—the author's intellectual work—is incapable of possession except as it is embodied in a tangible article, such as a statuette or a sheet of music.

The tangible articles containing the work may be in the possession of many persons other than the copyright owner, and they may use the work for their own enjoyment, but copyright restrains them from reproducing the work without the owner's consent.

Copyright as a Personal Right

Some commentators, particularly in European countries, have characterized copyright as a personal right of the author, or as a combination of personal and property rights.

It is true that an author's intellectual creation has the stamp of his personality and is identified with him; but since as his rights can be assigned to other persons and survive after his death, they are a unique kind of personal rights.

On the theory of personal right, some countries have included in their copyright laws special provisions for "moral rights" of authors. These provisions are intended to protect the author against certain specified acts injurious to his personal identity or reputation. They give the author the following rights:

To have his name appear on copies of his work.

To prevent the attribution to him of another person's work.

To prevent the reproduction of his work in a distorted or degrading form.

These moral rights are regarded as not assignable, but an author may sometimes agree to waive them in particular cases. In some countries the moral rights survive the author's death and may be enforced by his heirs or representatives.

In the United States the moral rights of authors have never been treated as aspects of copyright; but authors have been given much the same protection of personal rights under principles of the common law—such as those relating to implied contracts, unfair competition, misrepresentation, and defamation.

On the theory that copyright is essentially a personal right of the author, there is a tendency in some countries to declare that only the author or his heirs can own the copyright and that they cannot assign it. They may, however, give exclusive licenses to use the work, and the practical result is about the same as assignment.

The assignability of copyright has always been a fundamental feature of the law in the United States. To make copyright unassignable would conflict with the whole structure of the law and established practice. Our law, however, does limit assignments for the benefit of authors and their heirs by providing for the reversion to them of the right to renew the copyright beyond an initial term.

Copyright as a Monopoly

Copyright has sometimes been called a monopoly. This is true in the sense that the copyright owner is given exclusive control for a limited time over the market for his work.

On the other hand, any one work will ordinarily be competing in the market with many others; and copyright, by preventing mere duplication, tends to encourage the independent creation of competitive works. The real danger of monopoly arises only when many works of the same kind are pooled and controlled together.

Summary

Copyright is a legal device to give authors the exclusive right to exploit the market for their works. It has certain features of property rights, personal rights, and monopolies, but it is something apart from each of these. The legal principles usually applicable to property, personal rights, or monopolies are not always appropriate for copyright.

The primary purpose of copyright is to stimulate the creation and dissemination of intellectual works, thus advancing the progress of literature, science, and art. The grant of exclusive rights to authors is a dual means of achieving this end, and of compensating authors for their labors and their contributions to society.

SCOPE OF COPYRIGHT

The first copyright statute in this country was passed by the legislature of Connecticut in 1783 at the solicitation of Noah Webster, who wanted copyright protection for his spelling book. It is said that Mr. Webster then traveled through the rest of the Thirteen States and induced all except Delaware to enact similar statutes.

Thus, when the Convention met and formed the Constitution of the United States, copyright laws existed in twelve of the Thirteen States, but the requirements for copyright differed greatly —making it burdensome to an author seeking to protect his work. The need for a law which would be uniform and effective in all the states was so apparent that a provision was incorporated into the Constitution, as follows:

> Congress shall have power . . . to promote the progress of science and useful arts by securing for limited times to authors and inventors the exclusive right to their respective writings and discoveries.
> (Article I, Section 8.)

Our modern copyright law is based on this Constitutional provision.

The copyright legislation enacted in 1790 by the First Congress, which met shortly after the formation of the Constitution, gave protection only to maps, charts, and books. Since then, Congress and the courts have steadily expanded the meaning of the word "writing" to include many labors of the mind—thus giving effect to the purpose of the Constitution "to promote the progress of science and useful arts."

The concept of copyright has expanded in two directions:

> To cover other works of authorship, such as dramatic, musical, and art works.

> To grant exclusive rights to the copyright owner to disseminate the work by means other than printing—such as public performance and the making and distribution of sound recordings.

The "writings" thus far separately classified and protected under the copyright law are:

CLASS A: Books—including composite and cyclopedic works, directories, gazetteers, and other compilations.
CLASS B: Periodicals—including newspapers.

10

CLASS C: Lectures, sermons, addresses (prepared for oral delivery).

CLASS D: Dramatic or dramatico-musical compositions.

CLASS E: Musical compositions.

CLASS F: Maps.

CLASS G: Works of art; models or designs for works of art.

CLASS H: Reproductions of a work of art.

CLASS I: Drawings or plastic works of a scientific or technical character.

CLASS J: Photographs.

CLASS K: Prints and pictorial illustrations, including prints or labels used for articles of merchandise.

CLASS L: Motion-picture photoplays.

CLASS M: Motion pictures other than photoplays.

The copyright law states that these general classifications are not meant to limit the subject matter of copyright, which shall include *all the "writings"* of an author.

In other words, *every* production in the literary, scientific, and artistic domain is subject to copyright—whatever may be the mode or form of its expression, present or future—if it has originality of authorship.

It is up to Congress, however, to specify the expanding categories of copyrightable works.

HOW COPYRIGHT PROTECTS THE AUTHOR

The word "copyright" does not appear in the Constitution, nor is it expressly defined in the copyright law.

Copyright began by protecting against copying; but, as mentioned above, it has been expanded from its original concentration on the publishing right to include rights of translation, dramatization, public performance, and other rights in literary, dramatic, musical, and artistic works. Copyright is no longer a single right. It has become an aggregation or bundle of rights which might conveniently be referred to as "copyright" but is in reality many copyrights.

When one speaks of "copyright" today, he is speaking of certain *exclusive rights* granted by the copyright law.

These exclusive rights are:

To print, reprint, publish, copy, and sell the copyrighted work.

To translate the copyrighted work into other languages or dialects, or make any other version of it, if it is a literary work.

To dramatize it if it is a nondramatic work.

To convert it into a novel or other non-dramatic work if it is a drama.

To arrange or adapt it if it is a musical work.

To complete, execute, and finish it if it is a model or design for a work of art.

To deliver or authorize the delivery of the copyrighted work in public for profit if it is a lecture, sermon, address, or similar production.

To perform or represent the copyrighted work publicly if it is a drama; or if it is a dramatic work and not reproduced in copies for sale, to sell any manuscript or any record of it.

12

> To perform the copyrighted work publicly for profit if it is a musical composition;
>
> and
>
> For the purpose of public performance, to make any arrangement or setting of it—or of the melody of it—in any system of notation or any form of record in which the thought of an author may be recorded and from which it may be read or reproduced.

The copyright owner of a musical composition is also given the right under certain conditions to record or reproduce his composition on mechanical devices such as phonograph records.

WORKS SUBJECT TO COPYRIGHT
HOW THEY ARE COPYRIGHTED

General Standards

It is well established by a long line of court decisions that in order to be copyrightable a work must meet the following requirements:

> The work must be in the form of a "writing" —that is, it must be fixed in some tangible form from which it can be reproduced.
>
> The work must be a product of original creative authorship.

The works subject to copyright are divisible into two general groups—*published* and *unpublished*.

13

PUBLISHED WORKS

Some works are by their very nature intended for reproduction in multiple copies for sale or other public distribution. Books, including pamphlets, leaflets, stories, and schematic material; periodicals; maps; reproductions of works of art; and prints or pictorial illustrations are of this nature, and are *not copyrightable till they are published with notice of copyright.*

Publication with notice is a condition for copyright in the above-mentioned works. As a matter of fact, *it is the act of publication with notice that secures copyright protection.* After publication with notice, the claim to copyright must be registered in the Copyright Office.

It is impossible to overemphasize the importance of seeing that the requirements with respect to the copyright notice, both as to its form and position on the work, are strictly met. The existence of copyright itself depends on it, as the courts have ruled time after time. More copyrights have been lost by first publication without notice of copyright, or without proper notice, than by any other reason.

Thus, contrary to some belief, an author has the right to put the copyright notice on his published work *before* registering a claim. To repeat, he not only has the right, he must do so if he wishes to claim copyright. If he publishes the work without the notice, it amounts to a dedication to the public, and the work falls into the public domain and free use.

Some persons, on learning that works intended for public distribution are not copyrightable until published, undergo needless worries about the theft of their works while attempts are being made to market them. To protect their works, they register them with various guilds or unions; or, relying on an old wives' tale, send copies of their works to themselves by registered mail which they hold unopened. These measures do not provide any additional rights to an author. *Prior to publication, an author's*

14

rights in his unpublished works are fully protected under the common law. The common law forbids the copying, publication, or use of his unpublished works without his consent, and entitles him to damages for such injury.

How Published Works are Copyrighted

There are three important steps that must be taken to secure copyright in a published work:

1.

The work must be produced in copies with copyright notice. It must be produced in copies by printing or other means of re-production. It is *essential* that the copies bear a copyright notice.

2.

The work must be published. The word "published" is not to be confused with the above-mentioned word "produced." The copyright law defines the date of "publication" as the earliest date when copies of the first authorized edition were *placed on sale, sold, or otherwise publicly distributed.* The term of copyright starts running on this date.

3.

The claim must be registered. Promptly after publication, the claimant must submit to the Copyright Office a properly executed application form, two copies of the best edition of the work as published with notice, and a registration fee. With one exception, the registration fee for published works is four dollars. The fee for a commercial print or label is six dollars.

The Copyright Notice

Form of the Notice: As a general rule, the copyright notice consists of three elements:

1.

The word "Copyright;" the abbreviation "Copr.;" or the symbol ©.

2.

The name of the copyright owner.

3.

The year date of publication.

These three elements must appear together on the copies. For example:

Copyright 1962, by John Doe
or
Copr. 1962, by John Doe
or
© John Doe 1962

It is of special significance that a work by a United States national may be copyrighted so that protection is secured not only in the United States, but automatically as well in all of the several other countries that are parties to the Universal Copyright Convention. See page 56.

For published works of United States nationals it is necessary that all copies bear a particular form of copyright notice from the date of first publication. This notice consists of the symbol ©,

16

accompanied by the name of the copyright owner and the year date of publication—as in the above-given example.

By merely adding the phrase "All Rights Reserved" to the notice required by the Universal Copyright Convention, thus:

© **John Doe 1962**
All Rights Reserved

a United States citizen may secure automatic protection also in the countries that are parties to the Buenos Aires Convention. See page 60.

This is the most advantageous form of copyright notice. While the word "Copyright" and the abbreviation "Copr." are still accepted as legal parts of the copyright notice, a copyright applicant should, for the above-mentioned reasons, be especially aware of the far more advantageous use of the symbol © and the phrase "All Rights Reserved."

For a general discussion of copyright protection abroad for United States nationals, see pages 56-63.

Position of the Notice: The copyright notice in a book or other printed publication should appear on the title page or the page immediately following. The "page immediately following" is normally the reverse side of the page bearing the title.

The notice in a periodical should appear on the title page, on the first page of the text, or under the title heading.

The notice in a musical work should appear either on the title page or on the first page of music.

Optional Form of Notice for Graphic and Artistic Works: A special short form of notice is permissible for published graphic and artistic works registrable in CLASSES F through K; namely:

CLASS F: Maps.
CLASS G: Works of art; models or designs for works of art.
CLASS H: Reproductions of works of art.

CLASS I: Drawings or plastic works of a scientific or technical character.

CLASS J: Photographs.

CLASS K: Prints and pictorial illustrations, including prints or labels used for articles of merchandise.

This may consist of the symbol ©, accompanied by the initials, monogram, symbol or mark of the copyright owner, if the owner's name appears on some accessible portion of the work—such as the margin, back, base, pedestal, and the like. No year date is required.

The purpose of this is to prevent the marring of graphic and artistic works by detracting or obtrusive markings.

But here, again, if one wants to secure automatic copyright protection in the countries that are parties to the Universal Copyright Convention and the Buenos Aires Convention, the notice should be:

© John Doe 1962
All Rights Reserved

There can often be a real problem with regard to the placing of the copyright notice on graphic and artistic works. This is particularly true in regard to repetitive designs—copyrightable designs which are repeated on a continuous sheet or roll of paper, fabric, and the like.

In its 1914 decision in *Louis DeJonge and Company v. Breuker and Kessler Company,* the U. S. Supreme Court held that copyright in a painting which had been reproduced on wrapping paper was lost when twelve repetitions of the painting appeared on a sheet containing a single notice. This concept was upheld recently where a copyrighted chrysanthemum was applied repetitively to dress goods.

The problem of repetitive designs becomes still more difficult for certain types of works. For example, even if the notice for a wallpaper design is affixed to the selvedge often enough to satisfy the courts, there is a question as to the effect on copyright protection when the paper is applied to a wall and the selvedge is covered permanently.

No cases shed sufficient light on the problem of repetitive designs to determine how often the notice must be applied, or what happens when the notice is obliterated in actual use. If the doctrine of the *DeJonge* case is carried to its logical conclusion, it would appear difficult to protect repetitive designs without seriously detracting from the esthetic appearance of the product.

If one has doubts about the effective use of the copyright notice on a published graphic or artistic work, it would be wise to seek the advice of the Copyright Office *before publication.*

Optional Deposit of Copies

For certain classes of works, the Register of Copyrights may determine that it is impractical to deposit actual copies because of their size, weight, fragility, or high monetary value. In such cases, the law permits the filing of photographs or other identifying reproductions instead of the actual copies. Optional deposit is available for published works copyrightable in the following classes:

CLASS G: Works of art; models or designs for works of art.
CLASS H: Reproductions of works of art.
CLASS I: Drawings or plastic works of a scientific or technical character.
CLASS K: Prints and pictorial illustrations, including prints or labels used for articles of merchandise.

Generally, a copy is regarded as impractical for deposit if it is unsuited to the filing procedures of the Copyright Office. Most three-dimensional copies are regarded as impractical for deposit.

The option is not available, however, for fine prints and two-dimensional art reproductions. In all cases, the Register of Copyrights reserves the right to require deposit of actual copies.

The procedure to follow in taking advantage of the optional form of deposit is indicated on the application forms for the above classes, supplied free by the Copyright Office.

UNPUBLISHED WORKS

Although books, periodicals, reproductions of works of art, etc., just discussed, are not copyrightable in unpublished form, works which contain subject matter *primarily intended for performance or exhibition,* and which do not require reproduction in multiple copies in order to fulfill their purpose, may *voluntarily* be copyrighted as unpublished works.

Lectures or similar works prepared for oral delivery, dramatic compositions, music, works of art, drawings of a scientific or technical character, photographs, and motion pictures—all may be voluntarily copyrighted before reproduction for sales or other public distributions.

If an unpublished work under copyright is later reproduced in copies for sale or other public distribution, it must be copyrighted again as a published work, subject to the requirements of proper notice and deposit of copies.

If a work is voluntarily copyrighted in unpublished form, the term runs from the date it is registered in the Copyright Office —even if it is published later.

How Unpublished Works are Copyrighted

There are three requirements for securing copyright in an unpublished work:

1.

The claimant must submit a properly executed application form to the Copyright Office.

2.

Something must be deposited in the Office. The usual deposit is *one complete copy of the work.*

For works of art, however, a photograph of the work or some other identifying reproduction will suffice.

And for motion pictures, the following must be deposited: (1) the title of the film; (2) a description; (3) for photoplays, one print taken from each scene or act—and for other motion pictures, at least two prints taken from different sections of the film. The Register of Copyrights reserves the right to require deposit of complete films.

3.

The application and deposit must be accompanied by a registration fee of four dollars.

No copyright notice is required for unpublished works. The dividing line, however, between a preliminary distribution and the actual publication of a work may sometimes be difficult to determine. Therefore it is suggested that the owner may wish to affix notice of copyright to copies that are to be circulated beyond his control, to show that his interests in the work are reserved.

Under the terms of the Universal Copyright Convention, all unpublished works voluntarily copyrighted in the United States receive automatic copyright protection in all of the several other countries that are parties to the agreement. See page 58.

COMMON-LAW RIGHT VS. COPYRIGHT

It may be asked why, if an author's rights are protected under common law, he should bother to secure statutory copyright at all.

As we have seen, if the work is *intended for publication,* the author has no choice. He *must* copyright when publication takes place or lose the work to the public domain.

But if the work is *intended for performance or exhibition,* and does not require reproduction in multiple copies to fulfill its purpose, the author does have a choice between relying on the common law or securing voluntary copyright. If he elects to avail himself of copyright, he must abandon his common-law right. What are the comparative advantages?

At common law, the author or other owner may sue for infringement in a state court only; he must prove the validity of his work; and he must prove actual damages. His most important advantage is that, until publication, he has the common-law right *in perpetuity*—there is no limit to its duration as there is to copyright.

Voluntary copyright has many values. Registration provides an author or other owner with a permanent and official record of his copyright claim. It furnishes him with proof of the existence of his work at a particular time and the facts supporting his copyright claim. Particularly important to him is the certificate of registration, which is evidence without further proof of the stated facts and is generally accepted in trade circles as proof of copyright. He may sue for infringement in a federal court for a federal violation, and he is entitled to allowable damages when actual damages cannot well be determined. And, in addition to all these advantages, there is a special one: that of being entitled to automatic copyright protection in all of the several other countries that are parties to the Universal Copyright Convention. See page 58.

MATERIAL THAT CANNOT BE COPYRIGHTED

Names, Titles, and Slogans

The copyright law contains no provisions under which a monopoly in the use of a name or title, as such, can be secured.

Entry cannot be made in the Copyright Office for coined names, names of products, pen or stage names, or business names; or for the title, as such, of any literary, musical, dramatic, or other production apart from the work which it serves to identify.

Although titles may not, by themselves, be copyrighted, each work must be given some distinguishing title. Thus *the titles of books, music, dramas, and other works are recorded, but only in order to identify the works which are themselves the subject of copyright.*

Mere clauses or expressions, standing alone, are likewise not in themselves copyrightable, and do not become so because they constitute or lend themselves to a play upon words. Hence certain advertising announcements, slogans, mottoes, catch words, or the like, are not as a rule subject to copyright.

While names, titles, and slogans—as such—cannot be copyrighted, all may not be lost. In some circumstances, certain words, phrases, names, or titles may qualify for registration as trademarks. For trademark information, address the Commissioner of Patents, Washington 25, D.C.

Then, too, it must not be supposed that one whose work has become identified in the public mind under a distinctive name or title is at the mercy of any person who might seek to gain advantage by putting the name or title to his own use. Courts may be called upon to stop such practices under principles relating to unfair competition—all of which is quite apart from the limitations of the copyright law.

Ideas, Systems, Plans, and Methods

It is not possible to secure the exclusive right to a mere idea, system, plan, or method of doing anything.

It is the *expression* or *fulfillment* of an author's idea or ideas in some literary, scientific, or artistic form that is subject to copyright.

No matter how good an idea, system, plan, or method may be, the moment it is disclosed to the public it becomes common property; and the fact that the originator may have expended considerable effort, time, and money on it does not alter the situation.

Even if an idea, system, plan, or method were included along with other subject matter in a book which is protected by copyright, the copyright would not protect that portion of the book disclosing it.

The question is often asked: "Is there *any* way by which one may protect an idea, system, plan, or method?"

Apart from the lack of copyright protection, a disclosure of an idea, etc., may be made to others on a contractual basis— under such terms that misuse of the idea might become actionable as a breach of contract.

Also, certain systems, plans, or methods may qualify for patents. For information, address the Commissioner of Patents, Washington 25, D. C.

Standardized Forms

Music Forms
Blank Forms | Time Cards
Report Forms | Address Books
Graph Paper | Score Cards
Account Books | Order Books
Checks | And similar forms:

Such types of material, designed to record rather than convey information, are not considered original writings subject to copyright.

The same applies to standardized clauses in contracts, mortgages, deeds, leases, and other legal forms.

Furthermore, it is not possible to copyright works consisting entirely of information that is common property containing no original authorship. Works of this type would include, for example, standard calendars, height and weight charts, tape measures and rulers, schedules of sporting events, and lists or tables taken from public documents or other sources.

The main thing to remember, however, is that *copyright protects originality*. If you believe that any of the above-mentioned material created by you contains originality of artwork or other originality in addition to mere standardized qualities, state your case to the Copyright Office. It will inform you as to whether you may proceed with the registration of a claim to copyright.

Government Publications

United States Government publications are not copyrightable by reason of public policy.

The theory is that a government publication is made at public expense and consequently is the property of all.

This rule embraces generally all official documents, reports, bulletins, registers, and information circulars issued by various government agencies; also laws and court decisions.

But if a government publication includes copyrighted material issued by the government with the consent of a copyright owner, such material remains subject to copyright unless otherwise specified.

The common-law rulings denying copyright in the text of statutes, court decisions, official rulings and pronouncements, governmental proceedings, etc., are still deemed applicable to such materials emanating from the states and their political subdivisions; but no bar has been imposed on copyright in other publications of the state or local governments. Most of the states have enacted statutes for the securing of copyright in certain of their publications or in their publications generally.

Works in the Public Domain

No copyright can subsist in the original of any work which is in the public domain.

For a discussion of this, see pages 50-52.

Fraudulent, Libelous, Treasonable, Immoral or Obscene Works

Works of this nature are not copyrightable on the ground of public policy: they do not "promote the progress of science and useful arts."

The Copyright Office, however, does not inquire into the *merit* of any work submitted for copyright. Therefore it will not examine work to determine whether it may be fraudulent, libelous, treasonable, or immoral. It will record the claim to copyright and leave it to a court during some future infringement proceeding to decide whether the claim is valid.

If a court found a copyrighted work to be comprised of any of these undesirable qualities, it would declare the claim to copyright invalid and refuse to protect it.

It is in this sense that works of this nature are said to be non-copyrightable.

Games and Toys

Games and toys are not subject to copyright.

There are certain kinds of games and toys that may involve

the use of copyrightable material. For example, printed or picto-rial matter explaining or describing a game or toy may be copy-rightable as a "book." Also, artwork copyrightable in itself would continue to receive protection if employed in a game or toy. Such measures, however, would not secure protection for the idea or principle involved in the game or toy, nor for any mechanical devices for playing it.

Protection should be sought by patent.

Instruments, Tools, Utensils, So-Called "Gadgets," or Any Items of Functional Use

Articles designed for functional use are patentable, not copy-rightable.

As in the case of games and toys, above, printed or pictorial matter explaining the method of use of an instrument, tool, uten-sil, gadget, or similar article may be copyrightable as a "book," but the copyright would not protect any elements of invention inherent in the article.

Works of Applied Art

Copyright protects works of art and models or designs for works of art—but only in the realm of the fine arts, where works are intended primarily for esthetic or ornamental purposes. For a discussion of the problems of protection in the field of applied art, see pages 81-102.

Designs or Styles in Clothing

Copyright protects works of artistic craftsmanship as far as their form but not their utilitarian aspects are concerned. Conse-quently, *copyright is inadequate for the protection of designs or styles in clothing.* For a discussion of the problems of protection

27

in the field of applied art, including wearing apparel, see pages 81-102.

DURATION OF COPYRIGHT

The placing of time limits on the ownership of intangible intellectual property, while the ownership of tangible property is perpetual, is viewed by some commentators to be a historical hangover of a faulty legal distinction amounting to a burlesque on natural justice.

The fact is, however, that the placing of time limits on copyright is a worldwide practice; and the justification for it is based on public interest.

The United States provides two successive copyright terms totaling 56 years.

The initial term of copyright runs for 28 years.

If the work is copyrighted in *published* form, this term begins on the date of first publication. The date of publication is the earliest date when copies of the first authorized work were placed on sale, sold, or otherwise publicly distributed by the owner of the copyright or under his authority.

If the work is copyrighted in *unpublished* form, the term runs from the date it is registered in the Copyright Office—even if it is published later.

The copyright may be renewed for an additional term of 28 years upon application being filed in the last year of the first term.

The renewal term is not a continuation of the first term of copyright; it is actually a *new grant of copyright.*

Unless the copyright is renewed in the 28th year of the first term, it expires and the work falls into the public domain and free use.

In most foreign countries the term for works of an identified individual author runs for his life—or, if there is more than one

28

author, for the life of the last survivor—and a stated number of years after his death. For corporate or anonymous works, and also for works first published *after the author's death,* the term runs for a like number of years *after first publication.* The specified period varies in the foreign laws, ranging from 15 to 80 years —but the most prevalent pattern is a term expiring 50 years after the death of the author. Two countries, Nicaragua and Portugal, provide perpetual copyright.

Many persons have argued that our present maximum term of 56 years is too short.

It is true that a substantial number of works—though they make up a small percentage of all copyrighted works—continue to have commercial value beyond a 56-year period. In some of these cases, the author is still living or there are still dependents of a deceased author when the term expires.

Copyright Office experts agree that the protection provided at present is insufficient, and they believe that Congress should increase the maximum term from 56 to 76 years. With certain exceptions, the basic term would run for 28 years from first public dissemination of all works, and would be renewable for a second term of 48 years.

A maximum of 76 years would generally be equivalent to the term most prevalent in foreign countries; and if Congress votes the change, it would virtually assure protection for the author's lifetime, or if he dies prematurely, for his dependents during a reasonable period after his death.

COPYRIGHT OWNERSHIP

WHO MAY SECURE INITIAL COPYRIGHT

Copyright is an exclusive right based on authorship. Only an author or those deriving their rights through him may secure it.

An author's executors, administrators, or assigns may secure copyright:

> **If an author dies before securing copyright and leaves a will, the copyright may be secured by his executor.**
>
> **If an author dies and leaves no will, the copyright may be secured by his administrator.**
>
> **An author who has not secured copyright in a work may assign his right to secure it.**

Copyright extends to the works of United States citizens and stateless persons alike. A stateless person is one who is not a citizen or subject of any country and is not living in the United States. He is entitled to copyright on the principle that he is stateless through no fault of his own and that the United States should not subject him to further injury.

It extends also to the works of alien authors—that is, citizens or subjects of foreign countries—under certain conditions. Protection differs as between the common law and the copyright law:

Common-law protection extends to the unpublished works of all authors, regardless of nationality.

Under the copyright law, however, the published works of foreign authors may be copyrighted only in the following cases:

> **When the alien author is living permanently in the United States with intent to become a citizen.**
>
> **When the author is a national of a country designated in a proclamation by the President.**
>
> **When the work is entitled to protection under the Universal Copyright Convention.**

For a discussion of the copyright relationships between foreign countries and the United States, turn to page 56.

While the right to secure copyright is vested initially in the author and any other claimant must acquire the right from him, this basic rule is subject to two qualifications:

Works Made for Hire

If the work is produced by an employee "for hire," the *employer* has the right to secure copyright. This is justified on several grounds:

> **The work is produced on behalf of the employer and under his direction.**
>
> **The employee is paid for the work.**
>
> **The employer, since he pays all the costs and bears all the risk of loss, should reap any gain.**

In the absence of an agreement to the contrary, the courts, however, have not generally regarded commissioned works as "made for hire."

Composite Works

If the work is composite or collective—such as a magazine or encyclopedia—the *publisher* has the right to secure copyright.

A publisher in this situation is called a *proprietor*.

A contribution to a composite work may be copyrighted separately in the name of the author by placing a separate copyright notice on the contribution, but this is not common practice.

In situations where a separate notice is not feasible, a contributing author who wishes to retain copyright may make a prior agreement with the publisher of the composite work, whereby the publisher, as proprietor, agrees to assign copyright in the contribution to the author following publication.

An artist, for example, may sell a drawing for publication in a magazine and retain copyright to it in this manner.

Such agreements are common, especially in the magazine world. By such arrangement, the publisher, as proprietor, holds the copyright in trust for the author till such time as it is actually assigned to him—usually six months after publication.

WHO MAY SECURE RENEWAL COPYRIGHT

It frequently happens that an author sells his copyright outright for a comparatively small sum. If the work proves to be a great success beyond the initial 28-year term, it should be the exclusive right of the author to take the 28-year renewal term.

The copyright law attempts to protect the author and his family against an unprofitable or improvident disposition of the copyright.

Except for posthumous works, composite works, and works made for hire—which may be renewed by the *owner* of the copyright at the time of renewal—the renewal copyright may be claimed only by the following persons:

The *author* of the work, if he is still living.

If the author is not living, his *widow* or *children* may claim renewal. (Notice that the privilege of renewal does not pass to the author's estate; nor may the author bequeath away the right to others if the above heirs are living.)

> If neither the author, his widow, nor any of his children are living, and the author left a will, the *author's executor* may claim renewal.

> If the author dies without leaving a will, and neither his widow nor any of his children are living, his *next of kin* may claim renewal.

How to Claim Renewal Copyright

As mentioned previously, application must be made during the last year of the initial 28-year term—measured from the *exact date* on which the copyright began.

In other words, the application and renewal fee of two dollars should not be submitted till after the end of the 27th year of the first term, and *they must be received in the Copyright Office in acceptable form before the end of the 28th year.* It is advisable, therefore, to submit the application and fee well in advance of the expiration date of the original term to permit the filing of a new application if the first one received is not acceptable. If no application and fee are received, or if they are received after the original term has expired, the work falls into the public domain and the copyright cannot be revived.

Application for renewal copyright should be filed on FORM R, which is supplied free by the Copyright Office on request. If the work to be renewed is a print or label used for articles of merchandise, application should be filed on FORM RR.

Advance Assignment of the Renewal Right

The question is often asked: "Is it possible for an author to assign away his future renewal right?"

The courts have held that an assignment of the future renewal right by an author is binding if he lives into the 28th year and renewal registration is then made in his name.

If the author dies before then, the advance assignment will fail.

Since the person entitled to renewal copyright cannot be ascertained till the 28th year, an advance assignment creates an uncertain situation.

A considerable amount of trafficking in the possible future renewal rights of authors and their prospective heirs has grown up. Thus, in practice, the reversionary feature of our present renewal system has largely failed to accomplish its primary purpose. It has also been the source of more confusion and litigation than any other provision in our copyright law.

RIGHTS INCIDENTAL TO COPYRIGHT

The right to renew for another term of 28 years is one of the rights incidental to copyright. Other incidental rights include:

> The right to assign the copyright or to license the use of any of its component parts.

> The right to stop piratical copies.

> The right to sue for infringement.

CO-OWNERSHIP OF COPYRIGHT

There are a number of situations in which two or more persons may become co-owners of the same rights in the same work:

> When two or more authors create a work in collaboration, they are usually co-owners of the rights in the first instance.

When an author transfers to another person an undivided share of his rights, he and that person become co-owners.

When an author transfers all his rights to two or more persons, they become co-owners.

When a deceased author has two or more heirs, they may succeed to his rights as co-owners.

When there are several persons (for example, an author's children) in the class of persons entitled to claim a renewal copyright, they take the renewal as co-owners.

Co-ownership must be distinguished from "divisibility." Divisibility refers to the ownership by different persons of different rights in a work; co-ownership means that two or more persons together own the same rights.

Rights of Co-Owners

The copyright law is silent as to the rights of co-owners among themselves and in relation to third persons.

The courts have held that in the absence of a contract between them, co-owners hold the copyright as tenants in common —that is, each owns an equal, undivided interest—and if one dies, his interest inures to his estate.

Any one of the several co-owners of a copyright may use the work or license a third person to use it—without the consent of the other owners—but he must share the profits with them.

One co-owner can, of course, assign his interest to a third person, who would then become a co-owner in his stead; but since any co-owner may use the work or license its use, no third person could acquire exclusive rights except by assignment from all the owners.

Joint Authorship

When two or more authors collaborate in creating a single work of joint authorship, they are initially co-owners of the work.

When two or more authors independently create separate works, each is the sole owner of his own work even though the works are used collectively.

A clear example of a joint work is a single musical composition written by two composers working together—their contributions being merged inseparably into a single whole. A clear example on the other side is that of several musical compositions written independently by different composers and published together in a book of music. Between these two extremes, however, there are many cases that are not so clear-cut.

The copyright law provides no basis for determining what constitutes a work of joint authorship. Until recently the courts have held rather consistently that the test is whether the authors collaborated with the *intention* of having their contributions combined into a single integrated work.

Thus, where the composer of music and the author of lyrics intended to have their contributions integrated as a song, the courts have held the song a joint work even though the music and lyrics could each be used separately.

The test of joint authorship has been thrown into some confusion by a new theory that first emerged in the *Melancholy Baby* case decided by the U. S. Second Court of Appeals in 1946, and was carried further in the *Twelfth Street Rag* case decided by the same court in 1955.

In the *Twelfth Street Rag* case the composer of a musical composition without words, written as an instrumental piece, had secured copyright on his composition and had assigned the copyright to a music publisher who later commissioned a lyricist to write words for the music. The two authors separately assigned their renewal rights to different publishers.

Though there was no collaboration between the authors, and the composer did not contemplate or consent to the addition of words to his music, the court held that the music and words together constituted a single work of joint authorship, so that the assignees of the two authors were co-owners of the renewal copyright in the song.

The theory of this decision is that a copyrighted work complete in itself (musical composition) will become a joint work if additions (lyrics) are made later by another author at the request of the copyright owner.

This is a sharp departure from the view previously held by the courts. It does not require that the composer and lyricist collaborate, or that the composer have any intention that his work be combined with that of the lyricist.

Copyright experts believe that the question of what constitutes a work of joint authorship should be clarified in the copyright law. They would not go as far as the *Twelfth Street Rag* decision, but would adopt the test laid down by the earlier line of cases: that a joint work is one created by two or more authors who *intend* to have their contributions joined together as a single work.

ASSIGNMENT OR TRANSFER OF COPYRIGHT

We have seen that the author, or other owner of the right to secure copyright, may transfer that right to another person.

Also, after a copyright has been secured, the copyright owner may transfer any or all of the rights embraced in copyright.

An author may even assign his rights in a future work which he promises to produce *within a specified time*.

An owner may assign the entire copyright, or he may grant an exclusive license of one or more of the several rights that make up copyright. For example, the copyright owner of a musical work may grant to a motion picture company the exclusive right to use the work in motion pictures, while retaining to himself all other performance and recording rights.

The copyright owner may also grant a nonexclusive license. This is a mere permit to use the work in the manner specified, and does not transfer ownership of any right.

Divisibility of Copyright

Transfers covering one right but not others are common in commercial practice.

These part-transfers are sometimes called "exclusive licenses" and sometimes "assignments."

In practical effect an exclusive license of a particular right, such as the right to use a musical work in motion pictures, is equivalent to an assignment of that right: the licensee acquires the right to the exclusion of everyone—including the licensor.

In certain situations, however, the courts have indicated that copyright is an indivisible unit and, consequently, that a transfer of some, but not all, of the rights that make up a copyright is merely a license—not an assignment.

This *theory of indivisibility* has created a number of troublesome problems:

> The copyright law provides for the recordation of "assignments" but is silent about the recordation of exclusive licenses and other part-transfers. It is now uncertain whether "assignment" includes an exclusive license or other transfer of less than all the rights that make up a copyright.

> Whether a part-transfer is considered an assignment or a license may determine whether the proceeds are taxed as capital gains or ordinary income. Recent rulings, reversing earlier ones, have generally treated a part-transfer as an assignment for tax purposes.

> The owner of a part-transfer cannot now sue for infringement of a right transferred to him unless he joins the owner of the rest of the copyright as a party to the suit.

This last—the necessity of joining the owner of the residual rights in an infringement suit—is particularly troublesome. Except when the validity of the copyright is challenged, he usually has no interest in the suit, and making him a party to the suit becomes a serious obstacle when he is out of the jurisdiction.

The legal concept of an indivisible copyright is not reflected in business dealings. Copyright experts call it fictitious, meaningless, and outmoded. They believe that the copyright owner should be allowed to assign any *one* or *more* of his rights without assigning the *entire* copyright. They believe, too, that a person who acquires a particular exclusive right should be able to sue in his own name alone for the infringement of it.

Execution and Recordation of Transfers

A recordation system for copyright transfers is necessary to enable a transferee to give notice to all third persons of the transfer to him, and to enable third persons to determine from the record who is the owner.

Records of copyright ownership are particularly important in view of the nature of copyright as a form of intangible and incorporeal property not capable of physical possession.

While the copyright law provides for the recordation of assignments only and is silent about the recordation of exclusive licenses and other part-transfers, it has been the practice of the Copyright Office to record all transfers of ownership, in whole or in part.

Since there is no way of predicting with any degree of accuracy whether a court will regard a particular transaction as an assignment or a license, it is safer to record part-transfers as well as entire assignments.

An assignment of copyright must be in writing and must be recorded in the Copyright Office within three calendar months after its execution in the United States, or within six calendar months if it is executed outside the United States—in default of which it is void as against any subsequent purchaser or mortgagee for a valuable consideration, without notice, whose assignment has been duly recorded.

Every assignment of copyright executed in a foreign country must be acknowledged by the assignor before a consular officer or secretary of legation of the United States authorized by law to administer oaths or perform notarial acts.

The Copyright Office does not provide any special forms on which assignments may be made.

The original instrument of assignment should be sent to the Copyright Office for recordation. If the original instrument is not available, a certified copy may be used. The Office uses the photostatic method of recording. After recording, the volume and page number of the assignment record is affixed to the document which is then returned by ordinary mail. If the sender wishes to have it returned by registered mail, the post office registry fee should be included in addition to the recording fee (see below).

After the recordation of the assignment, it is not necessary for the assignee to file application for registration of the copyright claim in his name nor deposit copies of the work, unless registration and deposit of the same work was not previously made by the assignor. The assignee may substitute his name for that of the assignor in the notice of copyright appearing in the work.

In addition to assignments, there are other types of instruments which, though not transferring ownership, have some bearing on the status of a copyright. The Copyright Office now receives and records a number of miscellaneous documents such as nonexclusive licenses, powers of attorney, employment agreements, publishing contracts, changes in names or titles, and court decrees.

The recordation of such instruments is not required, but copyright information thus imparted is often important to researchers and the practice is encouraged.

The recording fee for every assignment, agreement, or other paper not exceeding six pages is three dollars; for each additional page, 50 cents; for recording each title in excess of one in the paper recorded, 50 cents additional.

USE OF COPYRIGHTED WORKS

There is no sharp bound of separation between the permitted and forbidden uses of copyrighted works. The copyright law does not define infringement, and the courts have been reluctant to do so—choosing rather to decide each case on its own special facts and circumstances. Therefore the question, "How much can you use without violation?", has no definite answer.

Broadly speaking, the unauthorized copying of any *substantial* part of a work—done either precisely or with colorable changes—would be infringement. And mere acknowledgment of a copyrighted source may not be taken as a license for substantial use.

"Substantial" refers to *quality* as well as *quantity*. For example, the theme of a musical composition may be contained in a single sequence of short duration, and unauthorized reproduction of it, regardless of the number of bars, would undoubtedly be plagiarism.

'The courts have recognized that a copyrighted work is subject to "fair use" for the purpose of study, research, criticism, and review, and that it may be commented on and quoted without permission to the extent of making the comments intelligible. Here again it is not only the quantity but the quality of the part taken that may be the important factor—including the use to which it is put.

One must use his own best judgment when using copyrighted works—obtaining where necessary the advice of legal counsel. If there are any doubts, the safe course always is to secure beforehand the consent of the author or other owner for the contemplated use of his work; and if permission cannot be obtained, the work should be avoided.

REMEDIES FOR INFRINGEMENT

The civil remedies for copyright infringement are:

1.

The court in its discretion may enjoin the infringement.

2.

The infringer is liable for the actual damages suffered by the copyright owner, "as well as" the infringer's profits. Or, instead of a smaller sum of actual damages and profits, the court may award statutory (allowable) damages in an amount it deems just. This amount, with certain exceptions, is to be not less than $250 nor more than $5000.

In view of the depreciated value of the dollar, Copyright Office expert advisers believe the $5000 maximum should be raised to $10,000. They would retain the $250 minimum.

3.

The court may order the impounding, pending the action, of all articles alleged to be infringing, and may order the destruction of all infringing copies and devices for making them.

4.

In all suits, except those by or against the United States, full costs shall be allowed, and the court may award to the prevailing party a reasonable attorney's fee as part of the costs.

ACTUAL DAMAGES AND PROFITS

Liability of a wrongdoer for the *actual damages* suffered by the injured person is a traditional remedy for civil wrongs generally. Actual damages have been one of the remedies for copyright infringement since the beginning of United States copyright.

Liability for the *profits* derived from a wrongful act has also been recognized as a remedy for civil wrongs. The wrongdoer's profits may sometimes be a measure of the damages suffered by the injured person, or they may be awarded to prevent unjust enrichment.

At present there is some question as to whether the copyright owner is entitled to *both* damages and the infringer's profits. The few court decisions on this question do not seem to have settled the issue. The recovery of either damages or profits—whichever of the two is larger—would seem to be the more equitable rule.

STATUTORY DAMAGES

Statutory damages—stated amounts for which an infringer may be held liable as an alternative to actual damages—have also been one of the features of United States copyright from the beginning.

The need for this special remedy arises from the inadequacy of actual damages and profits in many cases:

1.

The value of a copyright is, by its nature, difficult to establish, and the loss caused by an infringement is equally hard to determine. As a result, actual damages are often conjectural, and may be impossible or prohibitively expensive to prove.

2.

In many cases, especially in those involving public performances, the only direct loss that could be proven is the amount of a license fee. An award of such an amount would be an invitation to infringe with no risk of loss to the infringer.

3.

The actual damages capable of proof are often less than the cost to the copyright owner of detecting and investigating infringements.

4.

An award of the infringer's profits would often be equally inadequate. There may have been little or no profit, or it may be impossible to compute the amount of profits. Frequently the profits will not be an adequate measure of the injury caused to the copyright owner.

In sum, statutory damages are intended to assure adequate compensation to the copyright owner for his injury, and to deter infringement.

When Statutory Damages Are Awarded

With certain exceptions, in the main not applicable to works of art and musical works, the amount of statutory damages ranges from $250 to $5000. Within that range, the court has discretion to award the sum it considers just. Thus:

1.

If actual damages and profits are both less than $250, the court must award at least $250 and may in its discretion award a higher sum up to $5000.

2.

If actual damages or profits are proven in some amount between $250 and $5000, the court in its discretion may award either the proven amount or any higher sum up to $5000.

3.

If actual damages or profits are proven in excess of $5000, the court will award the proven amount. Statutory damages are not applicable in this case.

Innocent Infringers

Innocent infringers are liable for at least the $250 minimum.

The basic principle that an innocent infringer is liable, except where he has been misled through some act or omission of the copyright owner, is firmly established in the copyright law. As between an innocent copyright owner and an innocent infringer, it has generally been agreed that the loss caused by the infringement should be borne by the latter.

The only purpose of awarding damages for an innocent infringement is to compensate the copyright owner. The other purpose of statutory damages—to deter infringement—is not present as to infringements innocently committed.

Multiple Infringements

The question arises: What sum might be awarded as statutory damages if a single series of events is held to constitute a number of infringements? For example, the manufacture and sale of several hundred or several thousand infringing statues might be deemed separate infringements.

The danger of exorbitant awards in multiple infringement cases is more theoretical than real. Courts have used the formula of multiplying the number of infringements by $250, but they have done so to reach a result they thought just. No court has felt constrained to use this formula where the resulting total was considered excessive.

Our present law contains a schedule of amounts for each infringing copy or performance—the amounts varying for different works. Works of art and musical works are listed as follows:

> **For a painting, statue, or sculpture, ten dollars for every infringing copy made or sold**

> by or found in the possession of the infringer
> or his agents or employees; for all other works
> of art, one dollar for every infringing copy.
>
> For a dramatico-musical or a choral or orches-
> tral composition, $100 for the first and $50
> for every subsequent infringing performance;
> for other musical compositions ten dollars for
> every infringing performance.

It is understood that this schedule is a mere guide that the courts might use in their discretion in fixing the sum to be awarded as statutory damages within the $250-$5000 range.

The schedule has not proved to be a useful guide, because the amounts are arbitrary and the number of infringing copies or performances is only one of many factors to be considered in assessing damages.

Infringement After Actual Notice

A court may exceed the $5000 maximum, with no limit speci-fied, in the case of "infringements occurring after the actual notice to a defendant, either by service of process in a suit or other written notice served upon him."

Some fear has been expressed that this might result in exorbitant awards.

This provision was apparently based on the supposition that any infringement occurring after actual notice would necessarily be willful.

The supposition is questionable. For example, a television network may receive a notice alleging infringement of a musical work on the eve of a scheduled broadcast when it is too late to defer the program pending an investigation of the claim.

The possibility that a court, in its discretion, might award statutory damages greatly exceeding the usual maximum, merely because a notice had been sent, seems remote. In the very few cases where statutory damages of more than $5000 were awarded, other factors such as willful infringement on a large scale were involved.

REMEDIES OTHER THAN DAMAGES AND PROFITS

Injunctions

The law provides simply that a copyright infringer shall be liable to an injunction restraining such infringements.

The court may temporarily enjoin the defendant while the suit is pending, or it may issue a permanent injunction when the rights of the parties have been decided.

An injunction, by preventing future injury to the plaintiff, is often the most effective remedy—particularly when the damages caused by the infringement cannot be accurately determined. In some situations, however, an injunction may be futile, as where the only injury contemplated has already occurred. In other cases, an injunction may be too harsh on the defendant. The courts, in the exercise of their discretion to issue or deny an injunction, balance the plaintiff's need against the consequences the defendant would suffer. The terms of an injunction are tailored to fit the pressing necessities of the particular case.

Impounding and Destruction of Infringing Articles

Articles alleged to infringe a copyright may be impounded during the pendency of the action, on such terms and conditions as the court may prescribe. The rules of the U. S. Supreme Court require that the plaintiff post a bond of at least twice the value of the articles before they may be impounded, to indemnify the defendant for his loss if the articles are later found not to be infringing.

The court may order an infringer to deliver on oath for destruction all the infringing copies or devices, as well as plates, molds, matrices, or other means for making such infringing copies. Destruction is ordered only after the court has determined that the articles are infringing.

Impounding and destruction are extraordinary remedies which are rather infrequently applied by the courts. Like injunctions they may be highly effective remedies in some cases, and may be unnecessary or unwarranted in others. These are matters for the court to consider in exercising its discretion.

COSTS AND ATTORNEY'S FEES

The law provides that in copyright suits full costs shall be allowed, and the court may award to the prevailing party a reasonable attorney's fee. The costs involved in an infringement action are usually relatively small; but the prosecution or defense of a copyright suit may entail a good deal of work and expense, and an award of attorney's fees can be quite substantial.

The discretionary power of the courts to require the losing party to pay a reasonable attorney's fee is intended to discourage unfounded suits and frivolous defenses.

CRIMINAL PROVISIONS

Willful Infringement for Profit

In addition to the civil remedies for infringement, discussed above, the copyright law provides criminal penalties against willful infringement for profit. It is a misdemeanor, punishable by fine, imprisonment, or both, to infringe a copyright willfully and for profit, or to aid and abet such infringement knowingly and willfully.

Copyright owners have ordinarily resorted to civil remedies, but they have occasionally invoked this criminal provision. The criminal penalties can be effective in deterring flagrant and repeated infringements.

USE OF WORKS IN PUBLIC DOMAIN

No copyright can subsist in the original of any literary, scientific, or artistic work that is in the public domain. If once a work falls into the public domain, it can never be restored to copyright status. Anyone is entitled to the free use of such material.

There is no official listing of works in the public domain— as such.

The sale or other public distribution of a work without a copyright notice amounts to a dedication to the public. It falls automatically into the public domain.

A copyrighted work falls into the public domain at the end of the first term of 28 years if not renewed for the allowable second term of 28 years.

A copyrighted work on which the copyright has been renewed falls into the public domain at the end of the second term. In the United States, 56 years is presently considered to be ample protection time, and the monopoly is brought to an end.

Publications of the United States Government are specifically denied copyright protection by the copyright law, and are considered to be in the public domain. The reasoning is that a government publication, having been made at public expense, is the property of everyone. Exception: If a government publication includes copyrighted material used by the government with the consent of the copyright owner, such material remains subject to copyright unless otherwise specified.

There is a great wealth of foreign works which were thrown into the public domain by the passage of the Copyright Act of 1909: Any work which was published in any foreign country but was not copyrighted in the United States before July 1, 1909, is declared by the Act to be non-copyrightable.

The Act also threw into the public domain a considerable number of foreign and domestic works which were published in this country, but which, for one reason or another, failed to meet the July 1, 1909, deadline for completion of copyright registration.

Although works in the public domain may be used by anyone and cannot be copyrighted, the copyright law provides that

Compilations	**Translations**
Abridgments	**Adaptations**
Dramatizations	**Arrangements**

and other versions of material in the public domain shall be regarded as *new works subject to copyright*.

This protection is afforded if such new works require selective skill and originality of authorship.

The copyright of any such new work, however, does not mean that the compiler, arranger, adapter, or other user has acquired any exclusive right to the use of the public domain material. Anyone may make his own compilation, arrangement, adaptation, or other version, using the same sources.

The copyright in a new version covers only the additions, changes, or other new material appearing for the first time in the work. There is no way to restore copyright protection for a work in the public domain—even by including it in a new version.

The normal way to determine whether any published work is under copyright in the United States is to look for the copyright notice on the copy itself. Unpublished works, however, are not required to carry copyright notices; therefore their status is not as easily determined. If you wish to make free use of a particular work but are in doubt as to whether or not the work is in the

51

public domain, you may request the Copyright Office to make a search of its records to ascertain whether any copyright registration has been made in connection with it.

For a search, the Copyright Office should be furnished with as much of the following information as possible: the class under which the work falls (as music, work of art, photograph, etc.), the title, the author, the copyright claimant, and the year date.

Before 1938, all registrations in the Copyright Office were indexed under the name of the copyright claimant. In certain classes (drama, music, and motion pictures), entries can be located under title. As for books, search can be made under the name of the author. A general index, including all classifications, under the copyright claimant and selected authors and titles is available covering the period since January 1, 1938.

There is a search fee for this service by the Copyright Office. On receipt of your request, a search fee will be estimated—the charge being set at the rate of three dollars per hour.

The Copyright Office does not give legal opinions as to the copyright or public domain status of works on which search reports are furnished; the reports give only the fact of record.

Special searches are required to provide information concerning assignments and other recorded documents relating to changes in ownership. This information is not included in search reports unless specifically requested.

If your concern is about using a particular title or name, a search of the Copyright Office records would be of little value. Copyright does not give exclusive rights to titles, and titles *as such* are not registered in the Copyright Office. Consequently, searches are not undertaken to determine whether stated titles or names are original. The records reveal many different works identified by the same or similar titles. See page 23.

REPRINTS AND NEW VERSIONS

Reprints

A mere reprint or other issue of a copyrighted work is not subject to a new copyright. The copyright secured in the original publication protects the reprint—providing the reprint bears the original notice of copyright.

But a new revised edition of a copyrighted work is subject to a new copyright if it contains substantially new copyrightable matter.

New Versions

A new version of a work in the public domain, or a new version of a copyrighted work which has been produced with the consent of the copyright owner is subject to copyright as a "new work."

Copyrightable "new works" include

Compilations	Translations
Abridgments	Adaptations
Dramatizations	Arrangements

and other versions, as well as works republished with new matter.

Any work, to be copyrightable, must involve original, creative authorship. A new version must either be so different in substance from the original as to be regarded as a "new work," or it must contain an appreciable amount of new material. This new material must also be original and copyrightable in itself. When only a few slight variations or minor additions have been made, or when the revisions or added material consist solely of uncopyrightable elements, registration is not possible.

The Copyright Office, however, considers only the information contained in the application form in determining the registrability of the types of works discussed here; no attempt is made to compare the new version with a prior version of the work.

The copyright in a new version covers only the additions, changes, or other new material appearing for the first time in the work. There is no way to restore copyright protection for a work in the public domain, even by including it in a new version. And protection for a copyrighted work cannot be lengthened by republishing the work with new matter.

For a discussion on use of works in the public domain, see pages 50-52.

Notice of Copyright in Reprints and New Versions

The form of this notice is vitally important and may vary depending on the nature of the work. No general rule can cover all possible situations. If you intend to author a revised work or other new version, it would be wise to state your case to the Copyright Office and seek its advice concerning the proper notice to use.

RADIO AND TELEVISION PROGRAMS

The copyright law does not mention radio and television programs as such, and it is not possible to copyright the general idea, outline, title, or names of characters for a program or series. It is possible, however, to secure copyright protection for certain elements that go to make up the contents of a program.

Unpublished Scripts

The unpublished script of a program, or a group of related scripts comprising a series, may ordinarily be copyrighted in unpublished form.

If the script is nondramatic, such as a lecture, panel discussion, address, and the like, it may be copyrighted in CLASS C on APPLICATION FORM C.

If the work is in the form of a play, musical comedy, or similar "dramatic composition," it may be copyrighted in CLASS D on APPLICATION FORM D.

If there is a series of related programs, each script should contain a different episode number or issue date to distinguish it from the others.

To be copyrightable, a script must be more than an outline or format. It should be sufficiently developed so that a program could actually be produced from it.

Filmed Television Programs

A television program on film may be copyrighted as a motion picture. CLASS L, motion-picture photoplays, includes dramatic motion pictures such as features, serials, animated cartoons, musical plays, and similar works. CLASS M, motion pictures other than photoplays, includes nondramatic motion pictures such as newsreels, musical shorts, travelogs, educational films, and works of a similar nature. To secure copyright in these classes, use APPLICATION FORM L-M.

Other Elements of a Program

In addition to scripts and television films, various parts of a radio or television program may be copyrighted under one or more of the specific classes provided in the copyright law. For example, musical compositions may be copyrighted in CLASS E; works of art in CLASSES G and H; and photographs in CLASS J.

It is important that *any* copyrighted material included in a radio or television program is used only with the consent of the copyright owner.

Published Works

A published work under copyright, such as a novel, short story, play, musical composition, etc., would have protection when presented in a version on radio or television.

Limitations on Copyright Coverage

There are many misconceptions as to the effect of copyright registration for radio and television materials.

As mentioned before, the general idea, outline, title, or names of characters of a television program cannot be copyrighted. In some circumstances it may be possible for titles, ideas, and characters to be protected under the general law of unfair competition, but this has nothing to do with copyright. It is also important to know that a copyright registration extends only to the material deposited in the Copyright Office. Registration for a script covers the material in that script, but does not give any sort of "blanket" protection to future scripts or to a series as a whole.

INTERNATIONAL COPYRIGHT

COPYRIGHT PROTECTION ABROAD FOR UNITED STATES CITIZENS

Copyright protection for works of United States citizens may be obtained in the great majority of foreign countries by virtue of conventions, treaties, or agreements, or legislative provisions of such countries.

THE UNIVERSAL COPYRIGHT CONVENTION (THE U.C.C.)

The U. C. C. is an international treaty to which the United States is a party. Its practical purpose is to simplify the international protection of creative works by reducing to a minimum the formalities required for securing copyright among participating countries.

The U. C. C. came into force in the United States on September 16, 1955. It should not be confused with the so-called "International (or Berne) Copyright Union" (to which the United States does not belong) or to the various Pan-American Copyright Conventions.

The U. C. C. has become the most important and effective means for the permanent establishment of reciprocal copyright protection between the United States and other countries.

Protection Under the U.C.C.

The U. C. C. requires a participating country to give the same protection to foreign works which meet the Convention requirement as it gives to its own domestic works. To qualify for protection under the Convention, a work must have been created by a national of a participating country, or must have been published for the first time in a participating country.

How to Secure Copyright Under the U.C.C.

Published Works. A work by a United States national may be copyrighted, by publication with notice, so that protection is secured both in the United States and in all of the other countries that are parties to the U. C. C.

For this result it is necessary that all published copies bear a particular form of copyright notice from the date of their first publication in this country. This notice consists of the symbol © accompanied by the name of the copyright owner and the year date of publication. Example:

© John Doe 1962

To secure copyright both in the United States and in U. C. C. participating countries, the notice should be placed in one of the positions specified in the United States copyright law. Following publication, the claim to United States copyright should be registered in the Copyright Office in the usual way.

Although United States authors or foreign authors domiciled in the United States must comply with the formalities of the United States copyright law to be protected here, they need only publish their works bearing the convention notice to be accorded, in all other contracting countries, the protection afforded under the laws of those countries.

Unpublished Works. Under the terms of the U. C. C. all unpublished works voluntarily copyrighted in the United States receive automatic copyright protection in all of the several other countries that are parties to the agreement. No copyright notice is required on unpublished works.

List of Contracting Countries

Andorra	Haiti	Mexico
Argentina	Holy See	Monaco
Austria	Iceland	Nicaragua
Brazil	India	Nigeria
Cambodia	Ireland	Pakistan
Chile	Israel	Philippines
Costa Rica	Italy	Portugal
Cuba	Japan	Spain
Czechoslovakia	Laos	Sweden
Denmark	Lebanon	Switzerland
Ecuador	Liberia	United Kingdom
France	Liechtenstein	United States
German Federal Republic	Luxembourg	of America

This list of contracting countries to the U. C. C. is a growing list. Denmark and Nigeria were the latest to join at the time of this writing, having made ratifications effective February 9, 1962, and February 14, 1962, respectively. The Copyright Office will supply free on request up-to-date information from time to time regarding new parties to the Convention.

Works of Foreign U.C.C. Nationals

The works of foreign nationals qualifying for United States copyright protection under the U. C. C. do not have to be registered and deposited in the United States Copyright Office. Unless the foreign owner of a United States copyright in a U. C. C. work wishes to bring suit for copyright infringement in a United States court, he is not required to register a claim during the *first* 28-year copyright term.

While registration of foreign U.C.C. works is not required, the following factors might well be considered in deciding whether or not to register a claim:

1.

No registration fee is required for foreign works if application is made within six months after first publication.

2.

Registration provides a permanent public record, which could make marketing the work in the United States easier and help to establish that the work was first published with the U.C.C. notice. The bibliographical information contained in the catalogs of the Copyright Office and The Library of Congress is widely disseminated both in the United States and many other countries.

3.

Registration for the original term may facilitate renewal for the second 28-year term, for which registration will still be necessary. The record will provide useful information, particularly in computing the time limit for filing the renewal application.

BUENOS AIRES COPYRIGHT CONVENTION

The United States has also adhered, with a number of the other American Republics, to the copyright convention signed at Buenos Aires, Argentina, in 1910.

Since this Convention is open to adherence only by Western Hemisphere republics, the nations of the Eastern Hemisphere and Canada (as a part of the British Empire) are excluded.

This Convention specifies that authors of any contracting country who have secured copyright in their own country will enjoy in the other countries the rights accorded by their respective legislation—providing the work to be copyrighted contains a statement indicating the reservation of the property right.

In practice, this reservation appears usually to take the form of either "All Rights Reserved," or "All Rights Reserved Under Pan American Copyright Convention."

List of Contracting Countries

Argentina	Haiti
Bolivia	Honduras
Brazil	Nicaragua
Chile	Panama
Colombia	Paraguay
Costa Rica	Peru
Dominican Republic	United States of America
Ecuador	Uruguay
Guatemala	

BILATERAL ARRANGEMENTS

The United States has over a long period entered into bilateral copyright relations with 39 foreign countries, most of which, however, have since adhered to the Universal Copyright Convention or the Buenos Aires Convention. Those which have not are:

Australia	Greece	Poland
Canada	Hungary	Rumania
China	Netherlands	Thailand (Siam)
El Salvador	New Zealand	Tunis
Finland	Norway	Union of South Africa

In some of these foreign countries, particularly those that are not members of the Berne Union referred to below, United States authors who desire to secure copyright protection for their works may find it necessary to comply with the formalities required by the copyright law and administrative regulations of the particular country. As the requirements vary, anyone wishing to secure copyright protection in one of these countries may find it advantageous to consult an expert in the field or to secure the services of a representative in the particular foreign country to transact his copyright business there.

BERNE CONVENTIONS

A large number of countries (predominantly European and *not including the United States*) are members of the International Union for the Protection of Literary and Artistic Works—better known as the Berne Union, whose headquarters are at Berne, Switzerland.

Under the provisions of the several Berne Conventions, authors of any country belonging to the Union enjoy in the other countries the rights granted by such countries to their own citizens, with respect to their works whether unpublished or first published in any country of the Union.

61

Authors of a country *not* belonging to the Union (for example, the United States) may secure the rights granted by these conventions—providing they publish their works first or simultaneously in a country of the Union. The question, however, of what constitutes a *bona fide* first or simultaneous publication in a particular foreign country is a difficult legal one, and authors would do well to consult an expert in the field.

List of Berne Union Countries

Australia	Hungary	Norway
Austria	Iceland	Pakistan
Belgium	India	Philippines
Brazil	Indonesia	Poland
Bulgaria	Ireland	Portugal
Canada	Israel	Rumania
Czechoslovakia	Italy	Spain
Denmark	Japan	Sweden
Finland	Lebanon	Switzerland
France	Liechtenstein	Syria
Germany	Luxembourg	Thailand (Siam)
Great Britain and	Monaco	Tunisia
Northern Ireland	Morocco	Turkey
Greece	Netherlands	Union of South Africa
Holy See	New Zealand	Yugoslavia

The "Berne Union" is made up of countries adhering to one or more of the following: the original Berne Convention of 1886 and the successive revisions of Paris 1896, Berlin 1908, Rome 1928, and Brussels 1948.

Since different countries have different relationships under one or more of these, persons interested in obtaining detailed information, including application of the different provisions to territorial areas, should consult the Bureau de l'Union Internationale pour la Protection des Oeuvres Litteraires et Artistiques, Helvetiastrasse 7, Berne, Switzerland.

OTHER SOURCES OF PROTECTION

In addition to the countries with which the United States has established copyright relations, and apart from compliance with the provisions of the Berne Conventions, protection for United States works may be available in certain other countries under their domestic copyright laws.

The law of any such country should be examined to determine the existence and extent of possible protection, and it may be desirable in a particular instance to secure the advice of a lawyer or other person familiar with the foreign law and procedural requirements.

Part Two

ART COPYRIGHT

HOW COPYRIGHT PROTECTS ART

Copyright protects the *fine arts* in the broadest definition of the term, namely:

Painting	Poetry
Drawing	Music
Architecture	Dancing
Sculpture	and Dramatic Art

Artistic works may be protected under various copyright classifications:

CLASS A

BOOKS
(Published Works Only)

This class includes such publications as:

Books on the fine arts
Poems or songs without music
Art directories
Art catalogs
Composite works on art
Annual art publications
Alterations of artistic works such as
    Compilations
    Translations
    Abridgments
    Dramatizations
    Adaptations
    Arrangements

and similar text matter, with or without illustrations, published as a *book, pamphlet, folder, leaflet, card, single page,* or the like.

A broad meaning is given to the word "book." It is the intellectual production of the author which the copyright protects —not the particular physical form which the production ultimately takes—and the word "book" is to be understood not only in its technical sense of a bound volume, but as any kind of publication which the author selects to embody his artistic product.

A book may consist entirely of pictorial or illustrative matter, as well as compositions of words in readable form.

To Register a Claim in Class A:

For a book manufactured in the United States: Use APPLICATION FORM A.

For a book or periodical by a foreign author in a foreign language, manufactured outside the United States: Request APPLICATION FORM A-B FOREIGN and special instructions from the Copyright Office. (But see *Works of Foreign U.C.C. Nationals*, page 59.)

For a book or periodical in the English language, published outside the United States: Request APPLICATION FORM A-B AD INTERIM and special instructions from the Copyright Office.

CLASS B

PERIODICALS
(Published Works Only)

A periodical, as commonly understood, is a publication appearing at stated intervals, each number of which contains a variety of original articles by different authors.

Each number of a periodical is considered to be an independent publication. The copyright of a periodical protects all the copyrightable component parts of it.

Periodicals as a class include:

> Magazines about the fine arts
> Art reviews
> Art bulletins
> Proceedings of art societies

and similar publications, which appear at *regular intervals of less than a year.*

Copyright is also available in this class for a *Contribution to a Periodical.*

Advertisements of articles of merchandise published in magazines are not regarded as "contributions to periodicals." See CLASS K.

To Register a Claim in Class B:

For a periodical, use APPLICATION FORM B.
For a *Contribution to a Periodical,* use APPLICATION FORM BB.

CLASS C

LECTURES OR SIMILAR PRODUCTIONS PREPARED FOR ORAL DELIVERY
(Unpublished Works Only)

This class would include such works as:

> Art lectures, and recording scripts and scripts for radio and television art programs *not dramatic* in character.

These works, when published, become "books," and claims to copyright may be registered in CLASS A.

To Register a Claim in Class C:

Use APPLICATION FORM C.

CLASS D

DRAMATIC AND DRAMATICO-MUSICAL COMPOSITIONS

(Both Published and Unpublished Works)

The term "dramatic composition" includes the acting versions of:

> Plays for stage
> Motion-picture plays
> Plays designed for radio and television
> Pantomimes

and similar works dramatic in character.

The term "dramatico-musical composition" includes:

> Ballets   Operettas
> Operas   Musical plays

and similar productions. Choreographic works, dramatic in concept or idea and complete enough for performance without further development, may also be copyrighted in this class. But ballroom, social, and folk-dance steps are not copyrightable.

Dramatic and dramatico-musical compositions may be copyrighted in unpublished form; and, if published later, may be copyrighted again as published works.

A mere outline or synopsis of a dramatic composition will not suffice for the purpose of copyright in this class. The work submitted for copyright must be in dramatic form, substantially worked out as to dialogue, acting directions, stage directions, and other pertinent dramatic structures. It must be in such form that it is ready for performance without further, substantial development.

Scenarios in outline or synopsis form are classified as "books" and, if they are to be copyrighted, must first be published bearing notice of copyright.

The Copyright Office frequently receives letters in which the writer states that he has an idea for a new type of radio or television program, movie, opera, or the like, which he would like to copyright. *Mere dramatic ideas are not copyrightable.* It is the literary expression of the idea in the form of a particular dramatic composition that forms the subject matter of copyright, rather than the idea itself.

To Register a Claim in Class D:

For both published and unpublished works, use APPLICATION FORM D.

A Special Note on Choreographic Works:

Choreographic works, such as ballets, represent a recognized art form, and undoubtedly constitute works of authorship. Till fairly recent times it was difficult to secure copyright protection for choreographic works because of the absence of practical means of *fixing* them in a tangible form. Fixation is now feasible in the form of systems of notation recently developed, or in the form of motion pictures.

For purposes of copyright at least, the term "choreographic works" is understood to mean dance works created for presentation to an audience—thus excluding ballroom and other social dance steps designed merely for the personal enjoyment of the dancers. This distinction is important because *the copyright protection of choreographic works is concerned mainly with their public performance.*

Although not mentioned by name in the present copyright law, choreographic works have been regarded as copyrightable if they qualify as "dramatic compositions." There are some old court decisions indicating that a dance which presents a story or definite theme qualifies as a "dramatic" work.

71

The treatment of choreographic works as a species of "dramatic compositions" for copyright purposes has had two virtues: (1) It has served to define the protected choreographic works as dance works created for presentation to an audience; and (2) it has placed choreographic works in an existing category in which the rights of the copyright owner are established.

Treating choreographic works as a species of "dramatic compositions," however, has one serious shortcoming. Many choreographic works present "abstract" dance movements in which, aside from their esthetic appeal, no story or specific theme is readily apparent. Whether such abstract dances qualify as dramatic compositions is uncertain. The Copyright Office experts see no reason why an abstract dance, as an original creation of a choreographer's authorship, should not be protected as fully as a traditional ballet presenting a story or theme.

In view of the doubt as to whether abstract dances would come within the category of dramatic compositions, the experts have recommended that Congress designate choreographic works as a separate category of copyrightable works, and give them the same protection that is accorded dramatic compositions.

CLASS E

MUSICAL COMPOSITIONS
(Both Published and Unpublished Works)

See page 105.

CLASS F

MAPS
(Published Works Only)

This class includes all published cartographic representations of areas, such as:

> Terrestrial maps, atlases, and marine charts
> Celestial maps
> Three-dimensional works such as globes and
> relief models

Quasi-artistic works would be copyrightable in this class.

A map or group of maps accompanied by considerable descriptive matter may also be copyrighted as a "book," in CLASS A.

To Register a Claim in Class F:

Use FORM F.

CLASS G

WORKS OF ART; MODELS OR DESIGNS FOR WORKS OF ART
(Both Published and Unpublished Works)

Copyright protects pictorial, graphic, and sculptural works of artistic craftsmanship as far as their form but not their mechanical or utilitarian aspects are concerned.

This class includes such actual works of craftsmanship. A detailed list of works of art, or models and designs for works of art would probably be limitless. The copyright law does not attempt it. The works copyrightable in CLASS G are, generally:

1.

The fine arts intended solely for ornamental purposes—such as paintings in oil on canvas or other materials; mosaics; carvings and statuary in stone, metal, wood, etc.—in short, all works not generally susceptible of commercial reproduction.

73

2.

Objects of art, intended also for ornamental purposes, but unlike the above-mentioned works of art, usually reproduced in quantities for sale from the original—such as artistic jewelry, statuettes, vases, plaques, drawings, etchings, and the thousand and one articles passing under the name of bric-a-brac.

3.

Objects which serve primarily an ornamental, and incidentally a useful purpose—such as enamels, painted or stained glass windows, tapestries, and the like.

To Register a Claim in Class G:

For either a published or an unpublished work, use APPLICATION FORM G.

CLASS H

REPRODUCTIONS OF WORKS OF ART
(Published Works Only)

This class includes reproductions of existing works of art *in the same or a different medium*—such as a lithograph, photoengraving, etching, or drawing of a painting, sculpture, or other work of art.

To Register a Claim in Class H:

Use APPLICATION FORM H.

CLASS I

DRAWINGS OR PLASTIC WORKS
OF A SCIENTIFIC OR TECHNICAL CHARACTER
(Both Published and Unpublished Works)

This class includes:

Architectural drawings

Architectural Drawings and Structures

Architecture has traditionally been considered one of the arts, and the copyright laws of most countries provide specifically for copyright protection of "artistic" works of architecture—that is, artistic architectural *structures*—as well as plans, drawings, or models for architectural structures. In the United States, the protection now afforded to architectural works, particularly "artistic" structures, is somewhat uncertain and may be deemed too narrow.

"Architectural works" may be understood in a broad sense as referring to two different things: (1) the plans, drawings, or models for an architectural structure, and (2) the structure itself.

Architectural drawings are copyrightable under the present law within the general category of technical drawings. The copyright in an architectural drawing protects it against the unauthorized making and distribution of copies of the drawing.

When an architectural structure, such as a monument, is itself a "work of art," copyrighted drawings of the structure are protected against their "execution" by erecting the structure. This is merely an application of the copyright provision which protects "a model or design for a work of art" against its "execution." *But the courts have held that the drawings of a functional structure, which is not a "work of art," are not protected against their use in building the structure.*

Architectural structures themselves are not mentioned in the present copyright law. If a structure constitutes a "work of art"—for example, a piece of sculpture or an artistic monument—the structure itself may now be copyrighted under the general category of "works of art." But copyright protection is not available for functional structures that do not qualify as "works of art."

It seems clear that a structure designed solely for esthetic effect should be entitled to copyright protection on the same basis as any other nonutilitarian work of art. It seems equally clear, at the other extreme, that a functional structure having no artistic features is not an appropriate subject for copyright protection—even though it embodies original ideas as to technical methods of construction. The more difficult question is whether copyright protection should extend to structures that are functional in purpose but also display nonfunctional features of "artistic" design.

The Copyright Office experts are inclined to the view that a reasonable measure of protection should be afforded to the *designs* of functional structures. In the case of architecture particularly, it would often be difficult to differentiate between the functional and "artistic" features of a design. The experts do not believe that the copyright law provides the appropriate framework for their protection. They would leave this protection to be dealt with in the separate legislation proposed for the protection of ornamental designs of useful articles. See *Works of Applied Art,* page 81.

It should be understood, of course, that a nonutilitarian work of art—such as a piece of sculpture or a mural—which is superimposed on a functional structure but retains its separate identity remains copyrightable as a work of art apart from the structure.

To Register a Claim in Class I:

For either published or unpublished works, use APPLICATION FORM I.

CLASS J

PHOTOGRAPHS
(Both Published and Unpublished Works)

Art photography is copyrightable in this class, which includes:

Photographic prints
Filmstrips
Slide films
and individual slides

Photoengravings and other photomechanical reproductions of photographs—for example, postcards—are registrable in CLASS K.

To Register a Claim in Class J:

For either published or unpublished works, use APPLICATION FORM J.

CLASS K

PRINTS AND PICTORIAL ILLUSTRATIONS, INCLUDING PRINTS OR LABELS USED FOR ARTICLES OF MERCHANDISE
(Published Works Only)

This class includes:

Prints or pictorial illustrations
Greeting cards
Picture postcards

and similar prints produced by means of lithography, photoengraving, or other methods of reproduction.

77

A commercial print or label, not a trademark, published in connection with the sale or advertisement of an article of merchandise is also copyrightable in this class.

A claim to copyright cannot be registered in a commercial print or label consisting solely of trademark subject matter and lacking copyrightable matter. The Copyright Office will register a claim in a commercial print or label that contains the qualifications for copyright even though there is a trademark on it. The registration of such a print or label, however, does not give the claimant trademark rights. Copyright and trademark are two different things, and the type of protection available under the trademark law cannot be obtained by copyright registration.

For trademark information, address the Commissioner of Patents, Washington 25, D. C.

To Register a Claim in Class K:

Use APPLICATION FORM K in all instances, except:
For a print or label used for an article of merchandise, use AP-PLICATION FORM KK.

CLASS L

MOTION-PICTURE PHOTOPLAYS
(Both Published and Unpublished Works)

This class includes motion pictures *dramatic* in character—such as features, serials, animated cartoons, musical plays, and similar productions intended for projection on a screen, or for transmission by television or other means.

Motion pictures in this class may also serve as fixed forms of choreographic works.

To Register a Claim in Class L:

For either published or unpublished works, use APPLICATION FORM L-M.

CLASS M

MOTION PICTURES OTHER THAN PHOTOPLAYS
(Both Published and Unpublished Works)

This class includes *nondramatic* motion pictures—such as newsreels, musical shorts, travelogs, educational and vocational guidance films, and similar productions intended for projection on a screen, or for transmission by television or other means.

The artwork appearing in such nondramatic films would be protected in this class.

To Register a Claim in Class M:

For either published or unpublished works, use APPLICATION FORM L-M.

CARTOONS AND COMIC STRIPS

There is no specific reference in the copyright law to cartoons and comic strips. Therefore it is necessary to fit them into one of the classes of copyrightable works. The correct classification and the procedure for securing copyright will vary, depending on the nature of the work and the form in which it is presented.

The following classes are appropriate for the registration of *both published and unpublished* cartoons and comic strips:

CLASS G, WORKS OF ART—Covers
most drawings and paintings.

CLASS J, PHOTOGRAPHS—Covers film-strips and similar works embodying cartoons.

CLASS L, MOTION PICTURES—Covers animated cartoons.

The following classes are appropriate for the copyrighting of *published works only*:

CLASS K, PRINTS AND PICTORIAL IL-LUSTRATIONS—Covers individual cartoons and comic strips separately published with notice of copyright.

CLASS B, CONTRIBUTIONS TO PERIOD-ICALS—Covers cartoons and comic strips published with their own notice of copyright in a magazine or newspaper.

CLASS K, COMMERCIAL PRINTS OR LABELS—Covers cartoons and comic strips published as advertisements.

CLASS B, PERIODICALS—Covers "comic books" published at regular intervals under a general title. In addition, some cartoon material is distributed in "book" form by feature syndicates, for practically simultaneous publication in various newspapers and magazines. If these "syndicate books" are distributed at regular intervals, copyright in CLASS B is appropriate.

> CLASS A, BOOKS—Covers "comic books" and "syndicate books" which are not published at regular intervals.

Limitations on Copyright Coverage

The general idea or title of a cartoon or comic strip, and the cartoon characters as such, cannot be copyrighted. Nor is there such a thing as a "blanket copyright" which would protect the idea for a series of cartoons or the series as a whole. Copyright in a particular drawing or print does not extend to later works depicting the same character or idea. Although copyright in a drawing or print gives the owner the exclusive right to make other versions of the work, each later version becomes a new subject for copyright.

WORKS OF APPLIED ART

While the protection given to works of fine art is adequate and clear, and requires no further discussion, the opposite is true of works of applied art.

There is an overwhelming public and art-world interest in the multifarious aspects of applied art in our present-day civilization. Applied art has become so important in our daily living that an entirely new body of federal legislation apart from patent and copyright law is now being devised to enhance our culture and to protect the creative genius of artists in this field. Let us take a penetrating look at this important, progressive movement:

Objects primarily designed for a useful purpose, but made ornamental to please the eye and gratify the taste—such as rugs, lighting fixtures, household furniture, wearing apparel, and the like, commonly called applied or industrial art—do not come within the protection of the copyright law.

81

Our patent laws provide for the granting of design patents to any person who has invented any *new*, original, and ornamental design for an article of merchandise; but *the usual case is that works of applied art do not have the sufficient quality of invention for protection by design patent.*

Hence designs are, in the main, not protected by either copyright or patent law.

The correction of this injustice, long overdue, is complicated by many elements of a practical, administrative, economic, and commercial character. The big problem here is how to retain for the artist the benefits of his creative genius without at the same time unduly restricting or hampering manufacture and trade.

THE APPLIED ART PROBLEM IN THE COPYRIGHT OFFICE

In recent years, an important problem has arisen as to whether ornamental designs of useful articles come within the category of copyrightable "works of art." In *Mazer v. Stein* (347 U. S. 201, 1954), the United States Supreme Court held that where a statuette had been copyrighted as a "work of art," its copyright protection was not lost or diminished because it was intended to be used, and was used, as a lamp base. An unauthorized maker of lamps, the bases of which were copies of the statuette, was held an infringer of the copyright.

Since the *Mazer* decision, the courts have sustained copyright claims in "works of art" embodied in costume jewelry, fabrics, toys, and dinnerware. Where this sudden emergence of copyright in the design area will lead, it is hard to say; but it is clear that under the *Mazer* decision, the area of design protection under the existing copyright law is considerably broadened, and that the problem in the Copyright Office is becoming a serious one.

In the light of the *Mazer* case, the Copyright Office has

registered a rapidly increasing number of claims in "works of art" that are embodied in useful articles—including fabrics, jewelry, lace, dishes, glassware, silverware, lamps, clocks, ashtrays, and the like. But there have also been a number of copyright claims in designs of useful articles that the Copyright Office has refused to register on the ground that they were not "works of art." The denial of registration for some of these claims has been challenged in court, and it can be expected that copyright claims in the design area will continue to grow.

The principal administrative problem now faced by the Copyright Office in this field derives from the impracticability of the deposit of useful articles for copyright registration, and the difficulties in determining whether or not they embody or constitute copyrightable "works of art."

The Copyright Office experts believe, as the Supreme Court held in the *Mazer* case, that the protection now accorded by the copyright law should continue to be available for "works of art" —that is, pictorial, graphic, and sculptural works—even after they have been employed as a design or decoration for a useful article. In the years since the *Mazer* decision, full protection under the copyright law has not proved inappropriate for "works of art" used as a design or decoration of useful articles.

They do not believe, however, that it would be appropriate to extend the copyright law to industrial designs as such—automobiles, sewing machines, wearing apparel, furniture, appliances, and the like. There is, in this area, a delicate balance between the need for protection on the part of those who originate and invest in a design, and the possible effect of protection, if over-extended, in restraining competition. The term of copyright—which is now up to 56 years and may be made even longer—is too long for ordinary design protection. And there are other fundamentals of the copyright law—the provisions on notice, deposit, registration, publication, and liability of innocent distributors of infringing articles, for example—that are not suitable for the entire range of industrial designs.

Consequently, the Copyright Office experts would favor the granting of reasonable protection against the copying of industrial designs under a separate *sui generis* law.

What, exactly, is the design problem; what are the effects of design piracy on our modern economic society; and what is being done to bring about the passage of design legislation?

In May, 1958, a small nucleus of industry representatives met in Washington, D. C., to form a central organization and clearing house for the many different industries and groups throughout the country who look to legislation as their only hope against piracy. Following a larger organizational meeting held in New York City in June, the group began active operations on July 1, 1958. It is known as The National Committee for Effective Design Legislation (NCEDL). *It operates with the assistance of advisers from the Copyright and Patent Offices.*

In addition to its organizational function, the NCEDL has undertaken to educate the public on the pressing need for a new design protection law. It is also performing the legislative work necessary for the introduction and enactment of such a law—in conjunction with the Coordinating Committee on Designs of the National Council of Patent Law Associations, which originally sponsored design legislation as early as 1952.

The membership of NCEDL represents a number of different industries and interests from various parts of the country. These include manufacturers and designers of items ranging from clocks to corsets, lighting fixtures to ladles, high fidelity sets to *haute couture*. It includes trade associations and designer groups of national scope as well as individual manufacturers, designers, and members of the bar from several states.

The NCEDL studies have resulted in the best summary of our national need of:

84

PROTECTION FOR DESIGNS

The Problem

A judge was recently faced with the task of determining whether a wrist watch can be considered a "work of art." His job was made no easier by the novel argument put forward by the designers of the watch: They contended that their creation must be considered a work of art because it was so difficult to tell time from the watch!

Most of us would agree that a product can be artistically or attractively designed and perform its function at the same time. This has long been the two-fold challenge to designers in such industries as furniture, wearing apparel, silverware, and textiles. But today consumers insist on a combination of utility and a pleasing appearance in almost every item they buy. There is an ever-increasing demand for articles which not only work but look attractive or distinctive as well.

Examples of this trend may be seen everywhere. All of us expect our autos to run, our refrigerators to cool, and our fly swatters to accomplish their missions—yet we find the following developments:

1.

A vice-president of the Ford Motor Company has stated that beauty of design had become as important as the functional value of an automobile. The Company has recently established a Fashion Trend Department.

2.

General Motors has commissioned the famous French artist, Jean Cocteau, to decorate some of its refrigerators, while Westinghouse has designed a wood-enclosed refrigerator to serve as a room-divider.

3.

The plastics industry reports that even fly swatters are among the many items produced by its members which have been subjected to "design piracy."

Design piracy consists of the unauthorized copying of the appearance of someone else's product. It thus amounts to appropriating artistic work which is commercially valuable to its creator. The practice of design piracy is rampant in many industries. It spreads malignantly as each industry becomes conscious of the importance of "dressing up" its goods.

The pirate relies on the proven success of another's venture. He undertakes no designing expense, and runs no risks as to popular approval of a design. He is therefore able to undersell the originator and usually tries to add to his profits by using inferior materials and workmanship. He obtains the design for unauthorized copying in many ways, but often merely sketches the competitor's product as it is displayed.

This practice is possible because of deficiencies in the present laws concerning patents, copyrights, and unfair competition. Experts in the field have long recognized the inadequacy of present laws and the need for new legislation giving effective protection to creative designs. A judge of the New York Supreme Court recently deplored the fact that under existing precedents he was unable to prevent the copying of an original design for a woman's dress. He had this to say in the course of his written opinion:

> "What must be made crystal clear despite this disposition is that . . . (it) implies no approval or condonation of a pernicious practice that warrants some legislative or judicial interdiction . . .

> "No compelling reasons exist for excepting the style creators from the application of the basic rules of fair and honest dealing . . . Surely there can be no serious quarrel with the proposition that one should be held to strict account for purloining the possessions of another, created and developed through exceptional talent and experience . . .
>
> "Some method must be devised to meet this urgency."

THE EFFECTS OF DESIGN PIRACY

Design Piracy is Harmful to the Designer

The United States Constitution devotes 27 of its few thousand words to the protection of authors and inventors. As a result, we have long had somewhat elaborate copyright and patent laws on the books. These laws, however, make some curious distinctions. For example, a sculptor who creates a cocker spaniel in plaster ("work of art") for purposes of reproduction and sale in a dime store may obtain a copyright which can give him up to 56 years of protection against anyone who copies his particular cocker spaniel. His art school classmate who designs the shape of household appliances or women's hats or a chair may be unable to obtain effective protection for a single day, once his creation is displayed.

The injustice to the designer of functional items, who is an important contributor to the American cultural scene, is immediately apparent. Let us examine some of the consequences he suffers from this situation, and how effective legal protection for his designs will reward his creative efforts.

Designers generally do not own their own facilities for manufacturing the products embodying their designs. They must sell

87

or license their designs to manufacturers either on an employment or free lance basis. Their remuneration, of course, depends on the value of their artistic product to the manufacturer. It is equally clear that the value of their product is sharply reduced by the fact that it is *their* product only till it is copied by someone else.

As long as a manufacturer is unable to purchase a design which, if popular, will inure to his benefit, he can afford to invest only a limited amount of money in securing better designs. Thus, under present conditions, the designer cannot be fully rewarded for his creativity and his ability to appeal to the public taste.

It has been suggested that the practice of copying produces opportunities for designers who must continually develop new designs to outrun the copyists. It will suffice here to note that any such opportunities which might be enjoyed in special situations by relatively small numbers of designers will hardly compare with the increased demand for designers at all levels, once the law requires each producer to do his own work.

Legal protection for designs would thus produce economic benefits to designers in the form of increased demand for their product as well as a more adequate reward for a good design. In addition, designers would be relieved of the degrading, wasteful, and troublesome practices forced upon them by widespread piracy. For example, in some industries designers devote considerable effort to producing consciously a design difficult to copy. And a designer of men's sport shirts recently assumed the unenviable burden of selling a "mystery shirt," sight unseen, because of his certainty that his original design would be destroyed by copying as soon as it was revealed. Others are faced with the unfortunate directive to copy the work of another designer with only such variation as will permit the otherwise reputable manufacturer to deny copying. Freed from burdens such as these, designers will be able to concentrate on creativity and enjoy its rewards.

Design Piracy is Harmful to the Manufacturer

The immediate financial loss inflicted by copying upon a manufacturer who introduces an original design is an incontrovertible fact. Although it is by no means the only harmful result felt by manufacturers, it is the most obvious.

A concrete example of this effect is offered by a recent survey of textile converters who specialize in printed designs:

> "Without exception, all of these converters have had some of their designs copied exactly in the past five years. In most cases the copy, insofar as the design and colors in the design are concerned, was an exact facsimile. The only discernible difference was that in most cases the quality of the fabric was inferior. Invariably the copyist sold his products at a considerably lower price either to the same customers with whom the originator dealt or their competitors. Without exception, the originator of the design was compelled immediately to stop production of that design and sell off at a loss whatever inventory he had to meet the price of the copyist."

The direct loss to such converters was estimated roughly at $3,000,000 per year. In the vinyl fabrics industry—an industry plagued by copying since it began creating new designs and new styles—pirating of individual designs has cost the originator anywhere from an estimated $100,000 to $500,000.

As indicated above, this loss is caused by the copyist's ability to undersell the originator by reason of: (1) the saving of designing expense; (2) the copying of only those designs which have proven popular; (3) the use of inferior workmanship and materials. It should also be noted that copying floods the market with the same design and thereby drastically reduces the life of the design. Even the copyist loses by reason of early public apathy toward the particular design and the fact that his copy is in turn copied by others.

The over-all effect of design piracy is to discourage not only creative designing but also higher standards of workmanship and quality, since the low standards of the copyist must be met in order to compete. Since all may use the same design, this factor drops out of competition. Thus, the originating manufacturer justifiably asks himself why he should undertake the risks and burdens of introducing original designs when he cannot effectively reap the benefits.

One more word about those manufacturers presently living off copying, since many of them, recognizing the ethical weakness of their position, do not make themselves known at airings of this problem. It is true that effective design protection would require some adjustments for such manufacturers. But the ingenuity, time and money they expend in copying could be channeled into original designing without loss of profit. Designing expense, when spread over the cost of the larger number of sales which design protection would permit, could well be absorbed. Under a system of protection, the copyist of today might be surprised at the capabilities of his own organization. He need no longer be deceived, as was at least one manufacturer who employed a "designer" merely to copy designs of others. The manufacturer was favorably impressed with a design presented to him (and actually created) by his designer, but was reluctant to take the chance of introducing it. The designer finally had to convince him by assuring him that it was copied from the successful design of a competitor.

Design Piracy is Harmful to the Distributor and Retailer

It must be admitted that in the past, retailers have often opposed legislation giving greater protection to designs. It is clear, however, that this opposition has generally been based on the fear that under such proposed legislation retailers would be held liable as infringers and harassed by lawsuits. Legislation has been drafted, however, with an appreciation of the problems of retailers and with provisions for solving them.

The present piracy situation places substantial burdens on distributors and retailers which effective protection would remove. No matter what price line a distributor offers, he finds that copies of items he markets are sold elsewhere, usually underselling his item. He must then cut his price, often to the point where he is selling his goods as distress merchandise. The customer who purchased from him is dissatisfied, both as a result of seeing the item elsewhere at a lower price and the erratic pricing policy of the distributor himself. Cancellations and returns from customers are forced on the distributor who attempts to shift the burden to the manufacturer—all with attendant difficulties and ill will.

The distributor today is not merely prevented from fully satisfying his customers by reason of the limited number of designs in a particular product presently available; he is also uncertain whether his investment in particular active designs will be undercut by cheaper copies. Under a system of design protection, retailers at all levels would be better able to anticipate their needs for an original design on a more reliable basis. Their merchandising and pricing policies could be determined by supply and demand rather than the salvage operations often forced upon them by design piracy.

Design Piracy is Harmful to the Supplier

The suppliers of cotton to the textile converter, wood to the furniture maker, and chemicals to the vinyl fabrics producer have an important stake in the fight for design protection. Suppliers have begun to recognize the link between the over-all prosperity and stability of their industry and their own particular well-being.

The growth of institutional advertising has emphasized the fact that the consumers of the end product of an industry are of vital importance to the entire industry. Moreover, removal of the instability and uncertainties caused by design piracy cannot help but produce a steadier flow from the supplier to the manufacturer. And with a greater number of designs being produced under conditions of confidence, over-all productivity should show a marked upswing. It is thus not surprising that the chairman of a leading cotton manufacturer, in urging the textile industry to realize its potentialities, emphasized "developing increasingly brilliant and original styles and designs" as well as the need for "proper scheduling of manufacturing and the most efficient and economic use of the men and machines available." Both of these objectives would be greatly aided by the elimination of design piracy.

Many suppliers of basic materials have themselves taken an active role in promoting and encouraging creative designs. Perusal of the national and trade press makes this abundantly clear. The Aluminum Company of America recently advertised candle holders in a national magazine, calling attention to "graceful aluminum that will inspire designs, textures, and colors" in great number. Moreover, interior design exhibits and the exhibits of architects are usually graced with offerings of such suppliers as U. S. Plywood, U. S. Rubber Company, and Reynolds Metal Company. Such promotion of creative American designs can receive no greater push than by the enactment of new federal legislation granting for the first time effective legal protection to original designs.

Design Piracy is Harmful to the Consumer

Before turning to the injurious effects of piracy on the consumer, it may be well to answer a question which could reasonably be asked: Will design protection raise the price the consumer pays for desirable designs?

This problem involves the products being offered by manufacturers who presently originate designs and those offered by the copyists. The price set by the originator, even if shielded from copying, should not be any higher and may even be lower than is the case today. This is borne out by experience with consumer items protected by design patents, as well as pricing of books such as low cost paper books covered by copyright. One reason for this result is the fact that no single design can be so popular as to be priced substantially out of line with competing designs. Moreover, the economic waste caused by piracy and presently shared by industry and the consumer would be removed. A manufacturer need not price his popular item for a quick "killing" in advance of its being copied. In addition, he can anticipate his needs more reliably and thus order supplies and gauge production schedules more efficiently. Since he can depend on a more certain period of protection, he can produce more items at a single time and effect economies which can be passed on to the consumer.

Under a system of reasonable protection of creative designs, the offerings of the present copyists could not immediately duplicate, as they do today, designs created by others. They could, of course, after the expiration of a term of protection for an original design, copy such designs. In addition, there will be every incentive to present-day copyists to offer original designs themselves— designs that are in style as well as popularly priced. The lack of such incentive today is illustrated by the recent claim of a textile manufacturer that he is the *first* American company to commission Swedish designers to create an inexpensive line of fabric designs. As indicated above, designing expenses will be spread over a great number of items. The result should be maintenance, and in some cases lowering, of the general price levels existing today.

Today the consumer is faced with confusion by the array of identical and near-identical copies of a design. He is often deceived as to the quality and workmanship of a design which has been copied from a well-advertised and higher-priced item. Moreover, no matter at what price level a consumer purchases, he has had the experience at least once in his shopping career of seeing the copy of an item he has purchased displayed at a lower price.

The consumer is shortchanged by the copyist in other ways: Since the copyist attempts to capitalize on a design already popular while others are waiting to copy from him, the variety of designs offered to the consumer is relatively limited. In being deprived of a wider choice, the consumer is being deprived of his own originality of selection.

It is difficult to believe that a consumer earnestly wishes to wear the exact dress, buy the identical wall lamp, or use the same kitchen clock as his or her neighbor. All of us wish to be stylish, but design piracy discourages individual expression of a general style trend. The shop girl hardly wishes to wear the "same" dress that a prominent socialite wore *if* everyone else is wearing the same dress. The consumer would prefer to buy designs which are right in style but a little different from his neighbors. And at least he wants to have the choice of buying something different. Today he does not have that choice.

We have traced the need for design protection from the viewpoints of the designer, manufacturer, distributor, retailer, supplier, and consumer. There are other points of view, including those of interested government agencies, the patent and copyright bar, the trade press, and labor. But how design piracy harms various groups should not obscure two fundamental points:

Design piracy is morally wrong,and it inhibits cultural growth in the United States.

In a comprehensive study of design piracy conducted under United States Government auspices over a quarter of a century ago, the authors observed that the unethical nature of design piracy was a point of agreement by all concerned. This is not surprising. American society generally condemns taking something created by another without his permission. This has been crystallized in our views of plagiarism of books, music, and drama, as well as painting, drawing, sculpture and other arts. We should not tolerate plagiarism of designs.

The cultural harm is equally serious:

The problems faced by the automobile industry in capturing the public fancy were in recent times of national urgency. Even today the unusual success of foreign-made cars remains somewhat puzzling. At least one prominent industrial designer has attributed this phenomenon in part to the tendency of American manufacturers to pounce upon and exhaust a particular design of appearance rather than emphasize an imaginative design of their own.

We find a similar situation in ladies fashions where we seem to be content to play second fiddle to Paris. Furniture manufacturers hope to enhance the sale of their wares by billing them as "Scandinavian modern." Imported chinaware is often considered particularly desirable.

The lack of effective legal protection for designs in this country reduces the incentive for producing creative designs. This has been repeatedly noted by manufacturers, designers, and other observers. It is clear that designers in the United States have the creative abilities to make the United States a leader rather than a follower. It is high time that they be given a real opportunity to do so.

95

THE PRESENT LAW DOES NOT PROVIDE
EFFECTIVE PROTECTION

Patents Are Too Difficult to Obtain,
Too Slow and Too Expensive

Basically there are two types of patents. The type usually thought of when one hears the word "patent" is a mechanical patent—a grant by the United States Government protecting the functional operation of a machine, manufacture, or process. In addition, there are patents protecting appearance. The latter are called design patents and differ from mechanical patents only with respect to length of protection—the term for mechanical patents is seventeen years, while design patents last for three-and-a-half, seven, or fourteen years, depending on whether the applicant chooses to pay a fee of ten, fifteen, or thirty dollars.

In order to qualify for a patent, an applicant must introduce something new to a particular field. But he must do more than merely take a step forward—it must be a large step. The contribution must be such that it was not "obvious" to those in the field. These requirements are what patent lawyers mean when they speak of "novelty" and "invention."

It is apparent that many attractive and successful designs in such fields as wearing apparel, kitchenware, automobiles, and furniture fail to meet these high standards. The results in the Patent Office and the courts have convinced designers and manufacturers that design patents are difficult to obtain and difficult to enforce. And even if the requirements were not so high, it is apparent that judgments about appearance must be highly objective and unpredictable.

In view of the requirement that a design be novel, a search of earlier designs must be conducted by the Patent Office before it can issue a patent. Till the patent is actually granted, the designer or manufacturer markets his design at his peril. The time lag, which can be many months, is thus crucial.

Finally, the over-all expense of design patents is much greater than the above-mentioned statutory fees. Even such fees must be multiplied by the number of designs introduced by a manufacturer each year. But, in addition, a manufacturer who decides to rely on a patent usually must first seek the advice of patent counsel. Thus the cost of a preliminary search and legal fees also add to the expenses of securing a design patent.

Copyright Protection for "Works of Art" Covers Only Relatively Few Designs, and Even Those Covered Receive a Type of Protection Which Does Not Fit the Situation

A copyright is not as difficult to obtain as a patent. The author need only originate the work himself—that is, refrain from copying from someone else's work or from the common fund of works known as the "public domain." And he can obtain a copyright not only for a book, play, or musical composition, but also for a "work of art."

Can the design of a useful article be considered a "work of art" as that term is used in the copyright law? This is a question which has been troubling the courts and the United States Copyright Office for some time. The answer is that sometimes such designs have been considered "works of art," but more often they have not.

Neither the courts nor the Copyright Office set themselves up as art critics. In fact, the function of the latter is much more restricted than that of the Patent Office. The Copyright Office merely examines claims to copyright to determine whether the work seems to fall within the subject matter declared copyrightable by Congress; it does not search, for example, to see whether the same work has been created by someone earlier or whether something offered as a "work of art" is a particularly good work of art. Nevertheless, this Office, as well as the courts in infringement suits, must decide whether Congress intended the particular work in question to be included within the protection of the copyright law.

The court referred to in the beginning of this discussion decided that the wrist watch there involved, although attractively designed, could not be deemed to fall within such protection. This follows a line of decisions; for example, a dress design cannot be considered a work of art.

A significant pronouncement in this field was made by the United States Supreme Court in 1954. The Court held that the usefulness of an article did not prevent its being a work of art; but the Court did not define what a work of art is.

Involved in this case was a human figure used as a lamp base. There can be little dispute that this traditional subject of sculpture must be considered a "work of art." But what of the many other designs which do not so clearly fall within this classification? The Copyright Office has taken the view that this decision does not offer any guide as to whether, for example, the shape of a chair or of an egg-beater is to fit within the category of a work of art. The Office thus finds itself without authority to register claims to a wide variety of designs of useful articles.

The 1954 Supreme Court decision has resulted in some expansion of copyright protection. For example, artistic drawings or paintings cannot be denied protection because they are used on textiles. But as to these relatively few designs, different problems arise. Thus, the very technical provisions requiring a copyright notice are poorly adapted to textiles and can result in unintended loss of protection. Moreover, the historic concern of the copyright law with books and other printed matter produce other inappropriate results. For example, innocent sellers of a pirated copy of a copyrighted textile design are liable as infringers and the term of protection can be as long as 56 years. Thus, from several points of view, copyright does not provide the answer for either effective or equitable protection of designs for useful articles.

The Common Law of Judicial Decisions Has Not and Cannot Fulfill the Need for Design Protection

Till a design has been made generally available in concrete form, it is considered "unpublished" and may in some instances be protected under certain judicial doctrines. Even in this limited area, designers have often found practical problems of proof and other uncertainties in enforcing these rights.

Once a design is placed on the market, common law offers almost no hope of protection. The doctrine of "unfair competition" ordinarily requires that the copied features of the design be closely associated with the originator and that the copyist has attempted to palm off his copy as an original. We know that this is not the usual case.

From time to time there are glimmerings of protection by courts which seek merely to prevent a "free ride." An earlier court decision which prevented the appropriation by one news service of the news gathered and published by a competitor has since been narrowly limited to the facts of that case, and most courts have shown a marked reluctance to apply this doctrine to design piracy.

One more word about the inadequacy of a judicial solution of this problem: Courts are not equipped with the resources or tools of the legislature. They cannot investigate the economic aspects of design piracy as can Congress. And a court which finds protection appropriate cannot as easily fashion the compromises required in an area such as this. Thus, a serious problem in leaving this question to the courts is the risk that a judge so disposed will accord protection without being able to prescribe a limitation on its duration or to provide other safeguards.

It should be noted that the problem of design protection is world-wide and that legislative solutions are being sought in a number of countries outside the United States. There is, in fact, interest in providing effective protection on the international level by means of a multilateral treaty. It is clear that legislation in the United States should be delayed no longer.

A PROGRAM TO SECURE DESIGN
PROTECTION IS WELL UNDER WAY

A series of special bills for separate protection of ornamental designs of useful articles have been presented to Congress during the past five years. The most recent bills—S.1884, H.R.6776, and H.R.6777, all identical—were introduced in the 87th Congress, 1st Session, May 1961. These bills, now under consideration, are the outgrowth of similar bills introduced in the 86th Congress, and are the result of a reconciliation of the differences between the earlier bills.

While the presently proposed design legislation differs from the copyright law in most of its details, it can generally be said to rest upon "copyright principles." Basically, this means two things:

1.

A design can be protected if it is the "original" creation of its author. An original design is one which has not been copied from someone else's work or from a design in the "public domain." The protected design need not meet any test of novelty or inventiveness. There is no requirement that the designer introduce something the world has never seen before, or that he create something that marks a recognized advance over previous designs in the field.

2.

The original designer is protected only against the unauthorized *copying* or *imitation* of the substance of his protected design. If such copying takes place, the copyist is not shielded by making slight variations. On the other hand, if the owner of a similar design can prove that his design was created independently, rather than through copying or imitation, no infringement has taken place.

Other key provisions of the proposed legislation may be summarized briefly as follows:

   I. DURATION OF PROTECTION:
      Five years, with an opportunity to renew for an additional five years.

  II. CONDITION OF PROTECTION:
      A. *Registration:* A claim to protection must be registered in a United States Government office before the design is made known to the trade or public, or within six months after it is made known.
      B. *Notice:* If the design is made known to the trade or public *before* registration, the design to be protected must bear a prescribed form of notice.
      Protection is not forfeited if the notice is omitted after registration, though omission may sharply limit the design owner's legal remedies against infringers.

 III. INFRINGEMENT:
      The design owner may generally recover from anyone who, without his authority purposefully makes or imports articles embodying a copy of the protected design. Merely selling copies constitutes infringement only under

the most limited circumstances.

IV. REMEDIES:

    A. Injunction.

    B. Damages, which the court may increase threefold.

    C. Possible forfeiture or destruction of all infringing articles, plates, molds, *et cetera.*

    D. Recovery of costs, and possibly attorney fees.

The proposed legislation attempts to fill the gap created by copyright and patent laws by fashioning a scheme of protection tailor-made to the needs of designs of useful articles. Ideas are borrowed from both of these bodies of law, but they are specially adapted. For example, a notice is to be affixed to the article, as under the copyright law, but without the rigid requirements detailed by that law. Criminal penalties are imposed for fraudulently obtained registration. Lessons have also been learned from prior legislative attempts in the United States. Foremost among these are the elimination or limitation of liability of retailers, motion picture producers, and periodical publishers.

While greatly encouraged by the substantial progress already made, the National Committee for Effective Design Legislation recognizes the ambitious task ahead. The Committee continues to seek to broaden its membership and welcomes the active, financial, and moral support of all groups and individuals interested in design protection. There is at long last cause for optimism, but time, money, energy, and initiative are still needed to complete the job. The Committee welcomes your participation in helping to make design protection a reality. Address the National Committee for Effective Design Legislation, 200 East 42nd Street, New York 17, New York.

Part Three

MUSIC COPYRIGHT

COPYRIGHT IN MUSICAL COMPOSITIONS

CLASS E

MUSICAL COMPOSITIONS
(Both Published and Unpublished Works)

A musical composition consists of music alone, or of words and music combined.

This class includes all musical compositions (other than dramatico-musical compositions), with or without words, as well as new versions of musical compositions—such as arrangements, adaptations, and editings.

Dramatico-musical compositions (musical plays) are copyrightable in either published or unpublished form in CLASS D. See page 70.

Sound recordings are not copyrightable. Phonograph records, tape recordings, and other recordings are not regarded as "copies" of the musical compositions reproduced on them. For purposes of copyright registration, the musical composition should be written in some form of legible notation. If the composition includes words, they should if possible be written beneath the notes to which they are sung.

A poem or song without music is classified in the copyright law as a "book" and cannot be copyrighted till published with copyright notice. It may be published separately as a leaflet. See CLASS A, pages 67-68. It may also be copyrighted as a Contribution to a Periodical if it bears a separate notice of copyright in the name of the author. See CLASS B, pages 68-69.

Titles or names of musical compositions are not copyrightable. For a discussion of this, see page 23.

To Register a Claim in Class E:

For a musical composition, the author of which is a citizen or

105

domiciliary of the United States, or which was first published in the United States: Use APPLICATION FORM E.

For a musical composition the author of which is not a citizen or domiciliary of the United States and which was not first published in the United States: Use APPLICATION FORM E-FOREIGN. (But see *Works of Foreign U.C.C. Nationals*, page 59.)

RIGHTS IN MUSIC

The copyright owner of a musical composition is given the following rights:

1.

To print, reprint, publish, copy, and sell the copyrighted work.

2.

To arrange or adapt it.

3.

To perform the copyrighted work in public *for profit;* and for the purpose of public performance, to make any arrangement or setting of it—or of the melody of it—in any system of notation or any form of record in which the thought of the author may be recorded and from which it may be read or reproduced.

Subsidiary Rights in Music

In the music industry, the prevailing custom is that copyright is secured in the name of the publisher. The publisher then holds the copyright in trust for the composer with respect to all rights or portions of rights not transferred to the publisher.

The music industry deals with a great variety of different and distinct rights. These may be outlined as follows:

1. Publication rights.

2. Nondramatic rights: This includes performances in hotels, restaurants, theaters, night clubs, dance halls, and the like—and also nondramatic use on radio and television.

3. Dramatic rights:
   (a) Use on stage or in vaudeville;
   (b) Dramatic use on radio;
   (c) Dramatic use in television.

4. Recording rights:
   (a) Reproduction on phonograph records;
   (b) Use on electrical transcriptions or other sound recordings.

5. Synchronization right: Use in motion pictures.

This listing is not complete. There are other specialized uses: for example, the "cavalcade" rights—which include the right to use snatches from one composition, all of another, and a combination of other compositions by the same author.

The music publisher exercises the publishing right and retains legal title to and contracts for the recording, synchronization, and grand performing rights. There is some question as to whether the publisher ever acquires the "small" performing rights since, in most instances, these are usually vested in a performing rights organization by virtue of contracts with the author.

An author or composer is commonly a member of the American Society of Composers, Authors and Publishers (ASCAP) or Broadcast Music, Inc. (BMI). Members of ASCAP execute an assignment vesting in ASCAP the right to license nondramatic public performances of the members' works, both in being and those to be created. BMI writers grant exclusive public perform-ance rights to the organization, both for existing works and those to be composed during the contract period.

For further information on performing rights organizations, see pages 120-122.

The composer may also be a member of the American Guild of Authors and Composers (formerly Songwriters Protective As-sociation), in which case he assigns to them the mechanical rights in all compositions, actual and potential. AGAC members also sign standard contracts with publishers subject to the provisions of the basic contracts between AGAC and the particular publisher, and subject to the existing agreements with the performing rights societies.

THE "FOR PROFIT" LIMITATION ON THE PERFORMANCE RIGHT

For musical works, the copyright law limits the copyright owner's performance right to public performances "for profit."

The phrase "for profit" has been construed in a number of court decisions and now has a fairly well-defined meaning.

A public performance may be "for profit" even though no admission fee is charged, if it is given in furtherance of a com-mercial enterprise. For example, the playing of music in a hotel or restaurant has been held "for profit" since its purpose is to attract patronage.

On the other hand, a public performance given by a chari-table, educational, or similar organization, with no motive of private gain, has been regarded as not "for profit," even though the performance was part of a fund-raising event.

The purpose of the "for profit" limitation is to strike a balance between the interests of the copyright owners and those of the public.

But in the case of dramatico-musical compositions, which are classed as dramatic works, the copyright owner's performance right extends to all public performances, whether for profit or not.

The reasons for this difference in treatment between dramatic and nondramatic works are:

> The audience at a nonprofit performance of a dramatic work is less likely to attend another performance than is the case with nondramatic works.

> Public performance is usually the main source of revenue from a dramatic work; in the case of nondramatic works, revenue is also available from the sale of copies and sound recordings.

> Dramatic works are not as readily or as frequently performed for charitable, educational, and similar purposes as are nondramatic works.

LIMITATION ON THE RIGHT TO MAKE RECORDINGS THE COMPULSORY LICENSE PRINCIPLE

The owner of copyright in a musical composition is also given the right to record or reproduce his composition on mechanical devices such as phonograph records, but only under the following conditions:

Once the copyright owner has permitted the musical work to be recorded, any other person has a right to make recordings of the work.

This person may adopt either one of two alternatives:

> He may negotiate a recording contract with the copyright owner, and record the composi-

tion under the terms specified in the agreement;

or,

He may use the compulsory licensing provisions of the copyright law, which do not require him to get permission from the copyright owner. Under these provisions, any person may make recordings of a musical work which has already been recorded, if he pays the copyright owner a "mechanical royalty" of two cents per composition on each record he manufactures.

The compulsory license provision applies only to the use of music. Recordings of readings of literary works, lectures, dramatic presentations, and dramatico-musical works do not fall within the provisions. Nor has the compulsory license been applicable to the recording of music in theatrical or television motion pictures. Also, this provision includes only musical compositions published and copyrighted after July 1, 1909; and it does not include the works of a foreign composer unless he is a citizen or subject of a country which grants similar mechanical rights to citizens of the United States, or unless he is a citizen of a country which is a party to the Universal Copyright Convention. See pages 56-63.

The compulsory license is relatively infrequent in American law. There is no such limitation in other areas of copyright.

This specific provision places three limitations on the contractual freedom of the owner of the copyright to a musical composition. It establishes limits on:

1.

The persons with whom he may refuse to contract;

2.

The times at which he may contract;

3.

The price at which he may contract.

Moreover, the copyright owner may not place any time limitation on the period during which the copyrighted property may be used, providing only that the two-cent royalty is paid.

That the subject of compulsory license is an extremely controversial one is obvious from the many bills that have been introduced from the 68th Congress to the present day, and the comparatively small number ever reported out of committee or voted on by either House.

For over fifty years the recording industry has relied on the compulsory license principle. Forms of licensing arrangements, royalty rate schedules, and other industry practices have been predicated on the compulsory license provision.

Explained briefly, the compulsory license principle found its way into the copyright law as a compromise at a time (1909) when there was a strong probability of a monopoly in the music recording business if the mechanical recording right were given to music composers without some restriction.

Whether this compromise was sound even in the light of the situation then existing has been greatly debated. At any rate, the situation today is substantially different.

Recording of music for home use has been moved from the days of primitive cylinders, disks, and paper rolls to the era of high-fidelity records and tapes at a retail level which has made the home use of phonographs commonplace and the distribution of records a $400 million annual retail business.

Radio broadcasting has opened up a new market for recorded music and has been a factor in the development of high-fidelity recordings since the 3500 radio stations have demanded more and better recordings for program purposes. Radio has multiplied the demand for recorded music and the high quality of music far beyond anything that was imagined in 1909.

The advent of television has multiplied each of these aspects of the music business still further. Over 400 operating television stations, and their joint programming through three major networks, have also acted to multiply the demand for recorded music —not only on recordings of sound alone but also through the use of music in both theatrical and television motion pictures used for broadcast.

Author and publisher groups are seeking to eliminate the compulsory license provision, while the recording companies are exerting every effort to maintain it.

Should the principle be retained or eliminated?

The compulsory license provisions are rather severe in their effect on the copyright owner. Once he exploits his right to record his music, he is deprived of control over further recordings. He cannot control their quality, nor can he select the persons who will make them. There have been many complaints of inferior recordings and of recordings by financially irresponsible persons. What is perhaps more important, the copyright law places a ceiling of two cents per record on the royalty he can obtain. In essence, the compulsory license permits *anyone indiscriminately* to make records of the copyright owner's music at the two-cent rate fixed in the copyright law.

In practice, the authors of musical works generally assign their recording and other rights to publishers, under an agreement for the division of royalties. In most instances, the record companies secure licenses from the publishers—thereby avoiding some of the mechanics of notice and accounting required by the law for exercise of the compulsory license. But the legal rate of two cents per record operates as a ceiling on the royalty rate paid —even with the first recording. For records of popular music, the royalty rate paid is commonly less than two cents.

As mentioned, the danger of a monopoly in the situation existing in 1909 was apparently the sole reason for the compulsory license. There are now hundreds of recording companies competing with one another, and the music available for recording is widely scattered among hundreds of competitive publishers. The market for recordings and the number and variety of compositions recorded have increased tremendously. The volume of music available for recording is immense and constantly growing. Much of the new music available remains unrecorded, and no one can foretell whether a recording of a particular composition will appeal to the public.

Author and publisher groups urge strenuously that since the compulsory license is no longer justified as an antimonopoly measure, it should now be eliminated. They argue that the fundamental principle of copyright—that the author is to have the exclusive right to control the commercial exploitation of his work —should apply to the recording of music, as it is applied to all other kinds of works and to other means of exploiting music.

Representatives of the record industry argue that even though the antimonopoly reason for the compulsory license is gone, there are now other reasons for retaining it. They contend that, by giving all record companies the opportunity to make records of the music recorded by any one company, the compulsory license is beneficial in the following respects:

> **It provides the public with a variety of recordings of any particular musical work, which might not be true if the copyright owner could give an exclusive license to one record company.**

113

It enables smaller record companies to compete with the larger ones by offering other recordings of the same music.

It benefits authors and publishers by giving their works public exposure through several different recordings—thereby increasing their revenue from royalties.

All of these asserted benefits flow from multiple recordings of a musical work by several companies under nonexclusive licenses, as opposed to a single recording by one company under an exclusive license.

The removal of the compulsory license, however, would not necessarily result in the granting of exclusive licenses. If it is true that authors and publishers benefit from multiple recordings, they would presumably seek to give nonexclusive licenses to several companies. It is a fact that in those foreign countries having no compulsory license, the recording of musical works is usually licensed nonexclusively to any reputable company.

It seems likely that in the absence of the compulsory license, multiple recordings would still be licensed nonexclusively. If so, the three benefits attributed to the compulsory license by the record industry would still exist, but with these differences: The author or publisher could refuse a license to a recorder whom he considered irresponsible or for a recording he considered undesirable; and the royalty rate would be fixed by free negotiation.

Even assuming that removal of the compulsory license would result in the granting of exclusive licenses, any loss of the three benefits flowing from multiple recordings would be offset by other considerations:

1.

The public now gets a variety of recordings of certain musical works because, when a record made by one company promises to be a hit, other companies make records of the same music. Under a regime of exclusive licenses, each company would have to record different music. While the public would not get several recordings of the same music, it would probably get recordings of a greater number and variety of musical works.

2.

A small record company may now make a competing record of a musical work from which a large company has made a prospective hit, but this also works the other way. Many hits are now originated by small companies, and their prospective hits are often smothered by records of the same music brought out by larger companies having better-known performers and greater promotional facilities. Under a regime of exclusive licenses, the companies would not compete with various recordings of the same music, but they would compete with recordings of different music. There is little danger that the large companies would get all the hits—in the popular field the number of compositions available for recording is virtually inexhaustible, and which of them may become hits is unpredictable.

3.

The authors and publishers believe they would benefit from removal of the compulsory license. They would no doubt take care of their own interests in deciding whether nonexclusive or exclusive licenses might be more profitable for those authors who have already achieved success. The possibility of granting an exclusive license might give new and unknown authors more opportunity to have their works recorded.

Representatives of the record industry have also argued that the enormous growth since 1909 in the volume of records manufactured and sold has proved the worth of the compulsory license. They point out that the record industry has prospered, authors and publishers have received more royalties, and the public has been supplied with more records of a better quality at a lower price. It is difficult to see why this expansion of the record industry—coincident with technical improvements and rising public demand—should be attributed to the compulsory license. Other entertainment industries have enjoyed a similar growth. And it is known that the record industry has also expanded in foreign countries where there is no compulsory license.

Removal of the compulsory license would very likely result in a royalty rate, fixed by free negotiation, of more than the present legal ceiling of two cents. The record companies would, of course, lose the advantage of the lower rate. The price of records to the public might be increased by a few cents, though this is not certain, since many factors enter into the pricing of records. If it is true that a freely-negotiated rate would exceed two cents, it may be concluded that the two-cent ceiling denies authors and publishers the compensation due them for the use of their works.

The fundamental principle of copyright is that the author should have the exclusive right to exploit the market for his work —except where this would conflict with the public interest. In the situation prevailing in 1909, the public interest seemed to require the compulsory license to forestall the danger of a monopoly in musical recordings. The compulsory license is no longer needed for that purpose, and there appears to be no other public interest that now requires its retention.

For these reasons, *the Copyright Office expert advisers are currently recommending to Congress the complete elimination of the compulsory license provisions.*

The experts recognize, however, that the present practices of the record industry are based on the compulsory license, and that its elimination would require some major adjustments and new contractual relationships. They therefore propose that the present compulsory license provisions be left in effect for one year after the new law is passed.

If Congress, after considering this highly controversial question, determines that the principle of the compulsory license should be retained, the advisers believe that substantial changes in behalf of composers and publishers should be made in the present provisions.

THE JUKEBOX PROBLEM

The copyright law provides: "The reproduction or rendition of a musical composition by or upon coin-operated machines shall not be deemed a public performance for profit unless a fee is charged for admission to the place where such reproduction or rendition occurs."

This exempts the operators of "jukeboxes" from any obligation to pay royalties for the public performance of music, though their operation is clearly for profit and the public pays for the performance!

The jukebox exemption is a historical anomaly. The exemption was placed in the law in 1909 at the last minute with virtually no discussion. The coin-operated machines of that day were apparently a novelty of little economic consequence. The jukebox industry is now among the largest commercial users of music with an annual gross revenue of over a half-billion dollars.

Bills to repeal or modify this exemption have been and are now before Congress, and have been the subject of repeated and exhaustive hearings. In the course of those hearings, *Copyright Office expert advisers to Congress have expressed their view that this exemption should be repealed, or at least should be replaced by a provision requiring jukebox operators to pay reasonable royalties.*

In 1958, the Senate Committee on the Judiciary recommended

117

enactment of a bill eliminating the jukebox exemption and providing for remedies against only the jukebox operator.

In testimony before a Subcommittee of the Senate Committee on the Judiciary in 1958, the late Arthur Fisher, then Register of Copyrights, stated that he and his predecessors supported repeal of the jukebox exemption because:

> "It is an unsound exemption inconsistent with the basic principles of copyright law of this country; inconsistent with the basic principle of copyright legislation in nearly every other country in the world; that it was rather accidentally adopted in 1909 in a distinctly different atmosphere and that the preferable thing to do would be to repeal it outright."

At a hearing before a Subcommittee of the House Committee on the Judiciary on a subsequent bill to eliminate the jukebox exemption (1959), Mr. Fisher pointed out that the industry's primary product was copyrighted music, that although the industry's annual gross receipts were conservatively estimated at $520 million, the producers of this music have received *nothing* for the commercial use of their product. He added:

> "I know no other situation in the American economy where anybody would dream of presenting such a picture . . . It is argued that the primary producer should get no increase or no direct payment until a business, led by five manufacturers who do a gross business up in the $50 millions or more in this field, gets paid out every expense, before the primary producer gets anything.
>
> "This is really an astonishing thing, and I say to you that that is the reason these hearings have gone on here year after year in the House and in the Senate. And until there is a

> sound solution on some compromise basis, I
> do not think a wrong like that will rest quietly,
> either internationally or domestically."

Mr. Fisher also observed:

> "I may say that to my knowledge, over
> 13 years now, I have not found one single
> person who has not got a direct economic
> interest who believes that this exemption is
> sound. I just submit that to you based on my
> own experience and observation. All the
> neutrals, all the third parties believe that an
> exemption in a statute is unsound which pro-
> vides that distributors need not pay perform-
> ance rights for the commodity distributed
> and performed."

The adverse effect of the jukebox exemption in the international field was summed up by Senator Thruston B. Morton, then
Assistant Secretary of State, in a letter to the then Chairman of
the Senate Committee on the Judiciary in support of S.590(1955):

> ". . . the change in the copyright law as
> proposed in the bill would also serve to re-
> move an inequity in our law which has been
> a source of irritation in our international
> copyright relations. The provision in our pres-
> ent law exempting the rendition of musical
> compositions in coin-operated machines from
> the payment of royalty fees deprives the copy-
> right owner of an important source of re-
> muneration and there are indications that
> the exemption continues to receive the criti-
> cism of copyright circles and author groups
> in foreign countries."

Thus the battle rages. Jukebox operators are the only users
of music for profit who are not obligated to pay royalties, and

there is no special reason for their exemption. No such exemption is made in any other country, except that in Canada the playing of music on jukeboxes comes within a general exemption of performances by means of a gramophone. A Canadian commission appointed to review its copyright law recently declared that the exemption of jukeboxes is not warranted, but that since the royalties collected in Canada would go mainly to copyright owners in the United States, the withdrawal of the exemption in Canada might await like action in our country.

The Copyright Office expert advisers feel that their recommendations for the elimination of the jukebox exemption have been as strongly put as possible, and that the matter is now directly up to Congress. Moreover, they believe that any congressional consideration of legislation proposed for this purpose should continue without awaiting any general revision of copyright law.

PERFORMING RIGHTS ORGANIZATIONS

In the United States, as in virtually every other major country, copyright owners have found it necessary as a practical matter to place their works in a pool for the licensing of public performances. Musical performances are given so widely that no one copyright owner could police all performances of his music or collect the royalties due him. And on the other hand, persons who give performances of many musical works—such as broadcasters —would find it impractical to obtain licenses from, and pay royalties to, each of the many copyright owners individually.

Organizations have therefore been formed to combine the musical compositions of many owners into a single catalog for which the organization issues performing licenses and collects royalties.

Inherent in any organization of this sort is the potential danger of monopolistic control and discrimination—both as to users seeking licenses and as to copyright owners seeking to participate. In this respect a performing rights organization is comparable to a public utility.

In most foreign countries there is only one performing rights organization, operated under some form of government control. In the United States there are now two principal performing rights organizations: the American Society of Composers, Authors, and Publishers (ASCAP); and Broadcast Music, Inc. (BMI). Between them they license the public performance of the great bulk of copyrighted music. A third organization, Society of European Stage Authors and Composers (SESAC), licenses a relatively small catalog of music.

ASCAP is a membership organization of music writers and publishers, started in 1914. In 1958 it had about 4600 writer- and 1100 publisher-members. Its gross revenue for 1960 was about $32 million. Its net revenue, after expenses, is distributed among its members—50 per cent to the writers and 50 per cent to the publishers.

BMI was organized in 1939 by the broadcasting industry as a counterweight to ASCAP. In 1958 it licensed the music of about 2600 publishers, many of whom were currently inactive, and a number of individual writers. Its gross revenue for 1960 was about $12 million. BMI is not intended to make a profit. Its royalty schedules are adjusted to produce the revenue needed to defray its expenses, establish a reserve, and make payments to publishers and writers at stipulated rates.

SESAC is a privately-owned corporation established in 1930. As of 1958 it licensed the music of 284 publishers with a catalog comprised largely of specialized varieties. It is operated for profit and makes payments to its publisher-members at stipulated rates. Its gross revenue is not known.

The copyright law makes no mention of performing rights organizations, nor is there any other federal law for their regulation. Nevertheless, there has been official recognition of the need for these organizations and of the necessity to guard against abuses of their monopolistic position. Antitrust proceedings by the Department of Justice resulted in the acceptance by ASCAP and BMI of consent decrees in 1941, and the ASCAP decree was amended in 1950 and 1960.

These consent decrees contain a variety of requirements designed to prevent discrimination in the licensing of public performances. In addition, the ASCAP decree provides that any user may petition the court to review its royalty rates, and contains provisions regulating its admission of members, its internal organization and voting structure, and its distribution of income.

The organization and activities of the performing rights organizations in the United States have been the object of much discussion and controversy in congressional hearings and in antitrust proceedings. It has been seriously questioned whether the antitrust procedure is the most appropriate or effective means of regulating their operations, and suggestions have been made that they should be regulated by an administrative agency under statutory provisions.

Whether performing rights organizations should be further regulated, and, if so, what is the appropriate method for their regulation, involve problems so large and complex that Copyright Office expert advisers believe Congress should make it a special subject of comprehensive study.

"NEIGHBORING RIGHTS" AND THE UNAUTHORIZED REPRODUCTION OF SOUND RECORDINGS

During the past few years there has been considerable discussion here and abroad how to provide some protection to performing artists and for record producers in their sound recordings.

It has been proposed that performers or record producers, or both, be given the right to prevent the unauthorized reproduction of their sound recordings. It has also been suggested that their rights might extend to the collection of royalties for the use of their recordings in broadcasts and other public performances.

These proposals have been the subject of a series of international meetings to consider the development of an international agreement to protect "neighboring rights"—so-called because they border or neighbor on copyright. Most recent was the International Convention for the Protection of Performers, Producers of Phonograms and Broadcasting Organizations—The Diplomatic Conference on Neighboring Rights, Rome, October 10-26, 1961.

There has been a reluctance in many countries to go ahead with neighboring rights recognition until an international agreement was drawn. Without a convention to set the standards, a hodge-podge of conflicting national laws could spring up to impede the use of foreign works.

The text developed at this Conference is the first to take note of neighboring rights on an international level, and tends to spur the whole movement for giving domestic effect to them.

The gist of the Rome agreement is uniform recognition of neighboring rights and the idea of national treatment—that is, one member nation must accord to the citizens of another the same rights given to its own nationals.

Complicating the agreement is the fact that it is an effort to wrap in one package not only performers' rights, but rights of broadcasters against the unauthorized use of their signals and rights of record makers against the pirating of their product.

At any rate, the Rome agreement, shaped pretty much in line with United States copyright interests by United States participation, has prepared the way for our own domestic study of these important issues.

Taking into account our past record of resistance to copyright change, the immediate prospect for the United States on the Rome agreement would appear to be lengthy deliberations and wait-and-see tactics.

Here is the present attitude of the Copyright Office experts on this subject: It is important to an understanding of the problems involved here to distinguish between:

> **The literary or musical composition of an author embodied in a recording;**
>
> **The recorded rendition of the performer; and**
>
> **The recording as a work in itself.**

All three elements are present in most recordings—but *only the author's composition is given copyright protection in the United States.* The laws of some foreign countries have provisions for the protection of the performer in his recorded rendition, or for the protection of the record producer in the sound recording as a work in itself. Provisions in the foreign laws usually appear as adjuncts to the copyright statute, but they frequently differ—as to the scope and duration of protection and in other respects—from the provision governing copyrighted works in general.

Unauthorized reproduction of sound recordings has reached serious proportions. While there are no copyright provisions in the United States protecting performers or record producers against the unauthorized reproduction of their sound recordings, several recent court decisions have accorded protection under common-law doctrines of literary property and unfair competition. The lack of any copyright specification of the rights of performers and record producers may be leading to establishment of common-law rights that are unlimited in scope and duration.

A bill aimed at combating the counterfeit of records—H.R. 11793, 87th Congress, Second Session—has been enacted into Public Law 87-773, effective October 9, 1962. This Law, passed with the approval of the Copyright Office, provides that

"Whoever knowingly and with fraudulent intent transports, causes to be transported, receives, sells, or offers for sale in interstate or foreign commerce any phonograph record, disk, wire, tape, film, or other article on which sounds are recorded, to which or upon which is stamped, pasted, or affixed any forged or counterfeited label, knowing the label to have been falsely made, forged or counterfeited, shall be fined not more than $1,000 or imprisoned not more than one year, or both."

These common-law decisions and criminal provisions all suggest that the present situation with respect to the unauthorized reproduction of sound recordings is unsatisfactory, and that more effective federal statutory protection should be accorded within appropriate limits.

While the copyright experts believe that the principles of the copyright law offer the most appropriate basis for this protection, there are many complex issues that have not yet crystallized sufficiently to permit the making of detailed recommendations to Congress. Among the unresolved questions are:

Should the rights be given to the performer or to the record producer—or both?

Should the requirements of the copyright law as to notice and deposit be applied to sound recordings?

For what length of time should protection be accorded?

Should duplication be permitted in some situations, such as the reproduction of records on tape for broadcasting or for educational or other nonprofit purposes?

These questions are now being studied.

INDEX

L

M

N

O

P

Paintings, 73
Pamphlets, 67
Pantomines, 70-71
Performing artists, 122-125
Performing rights
Dramatic, 108-109
Music, 106-109
Performing rights organization
(See under *Music*)
Periodicals, 68-69
Phonograph records, 109-120, 122-125
Photoengravings, 74
Photographic prints, 77
Photographs, 77
Photomechanical reproductions of photographs,
77
Phrases, 23
Pictorial illustrations, 77-78
Picture postcards, 77
Piracy (See: *Infringement of copyright*)
Piratical copies, right to stop, 34
Plagiarism (See: *Infringement of copyright*)
Plans, 24
Plaques, 74
Plastic works, 75
Plays
Motion-picture, 70-71
Radio, 70-71
Stage, 70-71
Television, 70-71
Poems without music, 67, 105
Poetry, 67
Postcards, 77
Prints & pictorial illustrations, 15, 19, 77-78
Proceedings of art societies, 68-69
Protection for designs, 85-102
Public domain, use of works in, 26, 50-52
Public performance of dramatic works, 108-109
Publication, definition of, 15, 28
Published works, 14-20

R

Radio and television programs, 54-56, 69
Recordation of assignments or transfers, 39-41
Recording industry, 109-117, 122-125
Recording rights in music, 109-117
Recording scripts, 69
Register of Copyrights, address of, 4
Registration of copyright, 4, 15, 20-21
Relief model maps, 72-73
Renewal copyright, 28-29, 32-34
Advance assignment, 33-34
Duration, 28
How to claim, 33
Who may secure, 32-33

Reprints and new versions of copyrighted
works, 53-54
Reproductions of works of art, 74
Reviews, art, 68-69
Rights of performing artists (See under *Music*)
Rights of record makers (See under *Music*)
Rights incidental to copyright, 34
Rome Convention on "neighboring rights," 123

S

Scenarios, 70-71
Sculptural works, 73
Sewing machines, 83
Silverware, 83
Single pages, 67
Slidefilms, 77
Slides, individual, 77
Slogans, 23
Social dances, 70
Society of European Stage Authors
& Composers (SESAC), 121
Songs without music, 67, 105
Songwriters Protective Association (SPA), 108
Sound recordings, unauthorized duplication of,
122-125
Stained glass windows, 74
Standardized forms, 24-25
Stateless authors, 30
Statuary, 73
Statuettes, 74
Statutory damages for infringement, 44-48
Subject matter of copyright, 10-11, 13-21, 67-79
Subsidiary rights in music, 106-108
Substantial use (See: *Use of copyrighted works*)
Systems, 24

T

Tapestries, 74
Television programs, 54-56, 69
Terrestrial maps, 72-73
Titles, 23
Tools, 27
Toys, 26-27
Trademarks, 23, 24, 78
Transfer of copyright, 37-41
Transfers, execution & recordation of, 39-41
Translations, 11, 12, 51, 53, 67
Treasonable works, 26
Twelfth Street Rag case (See under *Music*)

U

Unauthorized reproduction of sound recordings
(See under *Music*)
Universal Copyright Convention
(See under *International copyright*)
Unpublished works, 20-21
Use of copyrighted works, 41-42